GOD IS IN THE

SMALL STUFF

for your

FAMILY

GOD IS IN THE SMALL STUFF

for your

FAMILY

Bruce & Stan

PROMISE
PRESS
An Imprint of Barbour Publishing

Unless otherwise indicated, all Scripture quotations are taken from the *Holy Bible,* New Living Translation, copyright 1996. Used by permission of Tyndale House Publishers, Inc., Wheaton, Illinois 60189, USA. All rights reserved.

Scripture marked NIV is from the HOLY BIBLE: New International Version®. NIV®. Copyright © 1973, 1978, 1984 by International Bible Society. Used by permission of Zondervan Publishing House.

Scripture marked KJV is from the King James Version of the Bible.

Published by Promise Press, an imprint of Barbour Publishing, Inc., P.O. Box 719, Uhrichsville, Ohio 44683, http://www.barbourbooks.com

Member of the
Evangelical Christian
Publishers Association

Printed in the United States of America.

Contents

FAMILY FUN

FAMILY RELATIONSHIPS

FAMILY CHALLENGES

FAMILY IMPROVEMENT

FAMILY RESPONSIBILITY

ALL ABOUT BRUCE & STAN

INTRODUCTION

We have one purpose in writing this book: We want to encourage you to see how God is involved in the details of your life.

We know that you can appreciate God's existence when you see a beautiful sunset or a star-filled evening sky.

The heavens tell of the glory of God. The skies
display his marvelous craftsmanship.
PSALM 19:1

But God is more personal and intimate than that. He is not restricted to working in the atmosphere. He is the creator of the universe, but He also created *you*.

And we know you can sense His presence when miraculous events occasionally happen to you. . .like walking away unharmed from a car crash.

God is our refuge and strength, always ready to
help in times of trouble.
PSALM 46:1

But God is more active than that. He doesn't just pop in and out of your life. God is not for "emergency use only."

God is very real and very present in your everyday life. Not just in the outer reaches of the cosmos, but in your home. Not just in a crisis, but in the commonplace circumstances of your schedule. When you learn to perceive God from this perspective, then your life will be so much more fulfilling.

> *I know the Lord is always with me. I will not be shaken, for he is right beside me.*
>
> PSALM 16:8

There is no better place to find God in the details of your life than in your family. You know, the small stuff: the ordinary routines of parents and kids . . . the mundane schedule of jobs and school . . . and the boring activities of meals and chores. But when you see God involved in these situations, all of a sudden they aren't ordinary, mundane, or boring anymore.

> *You will show me the way of life, granting me the joy of your presence.*
>
> PSALM 16:11

This book contains fifty-two essays that reflect on God's involvement in the circumstances of your family. Don't expect to find any earth-shattering revelations in these essays. That's the whole point. They aren't about the spectacular; just the small stuff. Spectacular things don't happen very often, but the small stuff happens all the time. And when you begin to see God in the small stuff of your family life, then they will become spectacular.

We conclude each essay with a few "wise sayings." One of them may catch your attention. They are short and (hopefully) memorable, so maybe you can think about them during your day. They are just simple observations about your ordinary life and an extraordinary God.

God has a plan for you and your family, but you won't know that plan unless you know God. He is anxious for you to see Him in the small stuff of your family life so you can know Him better.

> *"For I know the plans I have for you," says the Lord. "They are plans for good and not for disaster, to give you a future and a hope. If you look for me in earnest, you will find me when you seek me. I will be found by you," says the Lord.*
> JEREMIAH 29:11, 13–14

Bruce & Stan

A good name is more desirable
than great riches.

Proverbs 22:1 NIV

FAMILY HERITAGE

ONE
FAMILY NAME

We live in a time when family names are not held in high regard. We're not saying that people are ashamed of their names. They just don't know much about their names, and therefore they don't take much pride in them.

It used to be that people were proud of being a Johnson or a Schmidt or a Gonzales. You honored your name because it carried great meaning for you and your family. These days names don't seem to make much of a difference.

There are reasons for this lack of enthusiasm for family names. For one, it's common now for families to have children with different last names (more about blended families later in the book). But this isn't the main reason, nor is it a very good one. The larger reason we don't take more pride in our family names is that we don't *know* our heritage, and we don't know the meaning of our name.

Recently parents have made more of an effort to teach their kids the meaning of their *first* names. For example, *Bruce* means "safe and secure," and *Stan* means "one of perseverance." Together, we are two of the most solid, ordinary, dependable yet boring guys you would ever want to meet.

It's your surname, or *last* name, however, that truly carries your heritage, so why not dig into the details of the history and the meaning of your family name? In the old days (we're talking really old, as in Bible times), your name would have been connected to a place (as in *Stan of Fresno*) or a trade (as in *Bruce the Lawyer*). You might have even been linked to another person (as in the *Son of Bruce*). Whatever the connection, it gave you a sense of place and belonging. It gave you a sense of pride.

You might have a godly heritage, which is something to be thankful for. Investigate it. Did your ancestors struggle for their religious freedom? How was your family involved in the church's history? Was one of your ancestors of the same name involved in some noble cause that left its mark? Dig up the details and talk about them with your children. Tell them the stories of their name.

When it comes to your name—whether it's your first or your last—you can either ignore it or live up to it. And if there isn't much to live up to, then determine to be the first in your family to bring honor to the family name.

…In the Small Stuff

- Show interest in the names of people.

- Find the oldest relatives with your surname and ask them to tell their story.

- Write a summary of the history of your family and give copies to anyone who might be interested.

- If you can, trace your heritage to the first person in your family who became a Christian.

- Organize family reunions as often as possible.

For you have heard my vows,
O God; you have given me the heritage
of those who fear your name.

Psalm 61:5 NIV

TWO

HERITAGE

It is getting tougher to pass wealth to your children. The IRS imposes gift and estate taxes. Your state may have inheritance taxes. And don't forget those pesky probate fees. It is enough to discourage you from dying. But these problems only apply to an *inheritance* you leave to your heirs. You will be better off, and so will your children, if you concentrate on the *heritage* that you will leave behind.

Don't confuse an inheritance with a heritage. Oh, sure, they are both left by ancestors to descendants. But the similarity stops there. An *inheritance* is tangible: It consists of assets and property that can be counted and collected. A *heritage*, however, is intangible: it takes the form of the qualities and values that are reflected in the character of a person's life.

When people think about what they will leave to their heirs, they often focus on the inheritance instead of the heritage. What a tragic mistake. Even though it has nothing to do with wealth, a heritage can be far more valuable than an inheritance:

* A family's heritage can provide a sense of stability and tranquillity that transcends the fluctuations of the stock market.

* A family's heritage can foster a moral and charitable spirit that can discern how to share an inheritance with those less fortunate.

* A family's heritage can reinforce a sense of priorities that gives meaning to life, whether the inheritance is large or small.

You may work a lifetime to accumulate an inheritance for your children. But all of your effort can be lost in a moment, during your lifetime or theirs, through financial reversals, economic downturns, or poor judgment. You have no guarantee that it will be put to good use, and it may even cause problems and fights among your children.

Instead of finances, make your greatest gift to your children a rich heritage of personal qualities such as integrity, joy, and spiritual sensitivity to God. Devote your time, energy, and creativity to teaching and modeling such qualities to your children. Preserve and promote these qualities within your family. This is the most valuable legacy you can leave to your children (and it is tax-free, too).

...IN THE SMALL STUFF

* Pity the poor children who receive a large inheritance instead of a rich heritage.

* An inheritance can improve the *conveniences* of life, but a heritage can improve the *character* of life.

* You have to die to give an inheritance, but you can add to your family's heritage each day that you live.

- An inheritance has to be divided and split among your children, but they each receive the full benefit of the heritage you leave behind.

- You remember your inheritance when you look at the bank book; you remember your heritage when you look at the photo album.

I plan to keep on reminding you of these things. . . .
I want you to remember them long after I am gone.

2 Peter 1:12,15

THREE
REMEMBRANCES

We have short memories. God can do great things for our families, but before too long we forget all about them. Suffering from this memory deficit syndrome, we find ourselves asking: "What has God done for me lately?"

You are more likely to remember the things God has done for your family if you find a way to memorialize them.

As Joshua led the Israelites to the Promised Land, the Jordan River blocked them. God worked a miracle and made the riverbed dry so they could cross. Once they had reached the other side, Joshua sent 12 men (one from each of the 12 tribes) back into the riverbed to retrieve large stones. These stones were then stacked as a memorial to God's miraculous provision. Joshua described the purpose of the memorial to the people of Israel with these words:

> *In the future, your children will ask, "What do these stones mean?" Then you can tell them, "This is where the Israelites crossed the Jordan on dry ground."*
>
> JOSHUA 4:21–22

Shouldn't we follow Joshua's example? Shouldn't we memorialize, in some fashion, those events when God's care and provision were particularly apparent?

Such events are more frequent than you might suspect. (That's because they escaped your memory so quickly.) But think through the past events of your family's life. You can see God at work without looking too hard: restored health from an injury or illness; a financial crisis averted; the safe trip; the new job; the healthy baby; all of those things you prayed about, and God answered, but you have since forgotten.

Should you stack a pile of stones on your front lawn to mark each event? Well, probably not, because mowing the grass would be so difficult. But a photograph on the refrigerator might serve as a reminder. Or you might want to keep a special calendar on which you can mark the days of God's unusual provisions so those events can be remembered on their anniversary dates.

Make an effort to remember God's continual provisions for your family. When you do, something interesting will happen. The more you remember what God has done in your lives in the past, the more you will see Him at work in your lives in the present.

…In the Small Stuff

- If you spend all of your time thinking about what God will do for you in the future, you'll forget what God has done for you in the past.

- God's provision deserves at least as much celebration as growing a year older.

- God remembers what He has done for you lately. Do you?

- If you are having a difficult time being thankful, the problem may be your memory.

- Take time to tell someone what God has done for you.

All our life is a celebration for us;
we are convinced, in fact,
that God is always everywhere.

Clement of Alexandria

FOUR
CELEBRATIONS

Celebrations are made for families. The very *purpose* of a celebration is to observe or honor a particular person or a special day. Take birthdays, for example, the most common family celebration. Birthdays make for great celebrations, for what better reason is there to celebrate than to honor someone's existence? That's what birthdays do. They mark in years how long you've been living. Isn't that great?

You need *people* to help celebrate birthdays. What good is celebrating alone? Of course, we all know that the reason we invite people to a birthday celebration is so that people will *praise* you by bringing you *presents* and sing you that stupid birthday song. Usually you have all of these *people* with their *praises* and *presents* gather at a particular *place*, whether it's your house or a pizza parlor, and when it's all said and done, you end up having a *party*.

Isn't that simple? It's a bunch of little details (conveniently beginning with the letter *p*) that add up to a celebration: purpose, people, praise, presents, place, and a party.

Birthdays aren't the only occasion for a family celebration. Any purpose will do, as long as it celebrates someone in the family—a good report card, a promotion at work, an anniversary, moving to a new house, a new family pet, or doing something heroic. This list of potential celebrations is as long as your imagination (and energy).

Spiritual celebrations are very important to your family as well, but we tend to overlook these because we think they're covered by special spiritual days, such as Christmas and Easter. We're not saying that you should overlook the public observance of religious holidays, but we think you can add deeper meaning by turning them into family celebrations.

For Christmas, don't rely on the church Christmas program and candlelight service to bring meaning to your family's Christmas celebration. Do some reading and discover how you can incorporate the traditional observance of Advent into your home.

For Easter, your family can participate in Lent, practiced

worldwide in Christian churches. This isn't a substitute for what your church may be celebrating but a personalizing of the celebration.

The most personal spiritual celebration you can observe is the spiritual birthday of each family member. What we mean by spiritual birthday is this: On what day did you and others in your family first invite Jesus Christ into your life? If you don't know of a specific day, choose a day that's close to the time and count that as your spiritual birthday. Just as your physical birthday commemorates how many years old you are, your spiritual birthday celebrates the number of years you have been a Christ-follower. What better *purpose* for a celebration can you have? What better reason is there for other *people* to *praise* God for your spiritual life? So choose a *place* and have a *party* (*presents* are certainly optional). Feel free to invite friends and family, who will see firsthand the power of God in the details of your life.

Can you imagine the effectiveness of a spiritual birthday celebration on children and teenagers in your family? As you affirm God's place in their lives, God will bless them as individuals and your family as a whole. God enjoys the praises of His people, especially when we tell Him how much we value what He has done for us.

- Capture your family celebrations in pictures.

- Don't let the presents become the most important part of your celebrations.

- Put Jesus at the center of every celebration.

- Celebrate His birth at Christmas.

- Celebrate His resurrection at Easter.

- Celebrate His goodness at Thanksgiving.

- Celebrate His life on your birthday.

- Celebrate His love on your spiritual birthday.

W ithout our traditions,
we would be as shaky as a fiddler on the roof.

Tevye

FIVE

TRADITIONS

Does your family seem splintered by a hectic schedule? Is the frantic pace at which you live fracturing your family relationships? Are you looking for a way to bring a sense of permanence, stability, and togetherness back to your family? Family traditions may be the solution.

A family tradition doesn't have to be spectacular or logistically complicated. Sometimes the best traditions are the simplest. A family tradition requires only two components to be successful: It must be celebrated regularly, and everyone in the family must make it a priority.

Think back to your own childhood. What do you remember? Was it spending Sunday nights with ice cream sundaes at the dinner table? Maybe it was going out as a family for doughnuts on Saturday mornings. Or for those of you who were more health conscious, it might have been a special family night to celebrate a good report card. Maybe it was a summer vacation at the same old rickety cabin each year. Perhaps it was always decorating the Christmas tree on the first Saturday after Thanksgiving, always watching *It's a Wonderful Life* (even though everyone in the family could recite the dialogue from memory).

We live in a fast-paced society. Our minds are often focused on where we are going next instead of what we are doing now. Quality moments with the family are at risk of being forgotten in the whirlpool of mundane activities. But family traditions extract us, at least momentarily, from our frantic lives. They provide a sense of stability and predictability. Most important, they provide that most precious commodity: *time*. Time to reconnect with each other; time to talk about things important or trivial; time to simply enjoy being with each other.

Your family will go through stages. An effective tradition in one stage may not work in another. Some traditions may survive; others may need to be replaced. Family traditions can't be forced. They usually happen without fanfare. All of a sudden, you'll find your family repeating a familiar pattern. Find those events and moments. Reinforce them. It will take creativity, energy, and commitment to protect your traditions from the competition of the "outside world," but your family is worth it.

…IN THE SMALL STUFF

- What you do in your family tradition is not as important as the fact that you do it together.

- Traditions create a scrapbook of memories in your mind.

- Family traditions with your children are your legacy to your grandchildren.

- Time is the best thing to spend on your family.

- Family traditions communicate values much more effectively than a lecture.

_____

$\mathbf{M}$ay those who come behind us
find us faithful.

_____

Jon Mohr

SIX

LEGACY

You live in a unique moment in your personal history. No one else but you has the opportunity to learn about and learn from those who came *before* you (that's your *heritage*), while at the same time no one else can determine how you can impact those who come *after* you (that's your *legacy*).

Make no mistake about it. You *will* leave a legacy. Aaron Burr, America's most famous traitor, left a legacy, one his descendants have had to live down (or live with) ever since. Even obscure people leave a legacy, which by definition is something you hand down to your descendants, whether it's your material possessions or your reputation.

It's not that every detail of your life is going to be laid

before your children, grandchildren, and so on like an open book (remember how difficult it is to gather information about your ancestors). It's the *way* you live and the way you influence your family that matter most.

If your way of living is self-centered and self-serving, then it's likely that your legacy will be tied to material things only: how much money you leave, what kind of furniture you hand down, that sort of thing. On the other hand, if your way of living centers on others and what you give of yourself to help their needs, then your legacy will be more intangible and enduring.

When it's all said and done, the greatest legacy you can leave is a life centered on God. In the Old Testament, here is what God told the children of Israel:

> *"Hear, O Israel! The Lord is our God, the Lord alone. And you must love the Lord your God with all your heart, all your soul, and all your strength. And you must commit yourselves wholeheartedly to these commands I am giving you today. Repeat them again and again to your children."*
> DEUTERONOMY 6:4–7

The same command applies to God's children today: We are to love God wholeheartedly and teach our children to do the same. That's the kind of legacy that will last for generations and please God into eternity.

...In the Small Stuff

- Sit down with your family and develop a family mission statement.

- As you teach your children how to love God, you will love Him more yourself.

- Live your life so that when you die, people will know that you

  —loved others clearly.

  —loved your family dearly.

  —loved God completely.

Happiness is to be found only in the home
where God is loved and honoured,
where each one loves, and helps,
and cares for the others.

Theophanes Venard

THE FAMILY HOME

SEVEN
HOUSE AND HOME

If there's one place we all long to go, it's home. There's no place like it. Home is sweet. Whether it's on the range, in the city, or on a tree-lined street in a small town, home is where our hearts can be found, even if we're miles away.

There's a reason why people want to go home, especially on holidays, birthdays, or any special time when family and friends have occasion to gather. They want to be with people who know them. Remember the popular television show set in a bar? It was the place "where everybody knows your name." We all want to go to a place like that, and most of all, we want it to be home.

A home is more than a house, but your sweet memories of home may center on a particular place (or several places if your family moved around a lot). And in that place, it's the small stuff you remember. The rooms and furniture, the tastes and the smells. Beyond the physical details of your house and home, you probably recall traditions and the things you did together as a family. Some of it was the everyday stuff all families do, but other activities were unique to your family.

As you recall the memories and details and traditions of the house and home you grew up in, think about the memories and details and traditions you are creating in your own home. That's right. *Creating.* A house is *made*, not born, and so is a home. What matters about the place where you live is what you put in it every day: the small stuff that will bring your family home long after they've left.

...IN THE SMALL STUFF

- A comfortable home is one that feels good to everyone, even strangers.

- As much as possible, make your home a place that honors God.

- A clutter-free home isn't necessarily a worry-free home.

- Cherish the sounds of your children while they are home; someday all you will hear is silence.

- Everyone will feel love if God is loved in your home.

The Christian home is the Master's workshop where the processes of character molding are silently, lovingly, faithfully and successfully carried on.

Richard Monckton Milnes

EIGHT
THE DINNER TABLE

Strategic decisions often come from obscure places. When the astronauts walked on the moon, they received their directions from a nondescript building in the humble city of Houston, Texas. One of the world's biggest computer companies started from a small room in a college dormitory. And so it is with your family. Great accomplishments and admirable character traits might be traced to an insignificant piece of furniture—your dinner table.

Oh, the table itself is irrelevant. It could be purchased from Ethan Allen or from Wards. It might be constructed with chrome and Formica, or from mahogany with chintz seat cushions. The significance of the dinner table is not how it was constructed, but how it is used. It was designed and purchased to provide your family with a place to eat dinner together. What happens in your family may depend on whether the table was actually used for that purpose.

Dinnertime is usually much more conducive to family dialogue than breakfast. You probably have at least one member of your family who isn't a "morning person." (Any attempt at meaningful conversation over cereal and toast will be rebuffed by grunts and glares or the sound of deep breathing resonating through the nasal passages.) Unless everybody is able to rise *and* shine with plenty of time for showering, dressing, eating, and commuting, a meaningful breakfast time will be futile.

Dinnertime is different. By sunset, most everybody is awake (although a few of us have been known to doze off immediately after staggering from the dinner table to the recliner). The challenge at dinner time is the coordination of schedules. The Allied forces invaded Normandy with less strategic planning than will be required to assemble your family around the dinner table at the same time. Parents have work agendas and appointments that seem incompatible; the children have after-school activities and evening commitments that conflict. But don't surrender in the face of such obstacles.

The time and effort required to gather your "troops" for dinner will be well rewarded.

The dinner table is the best place for family information. It is here that your family members can report on the events of their day: the victories; the defeats (or at least the discouragements if they aren't willing to admit the defeats); what's new; and what's going to happen in the future. The dinner dialogue is the family's way of staying current with what's going on in each others' lives.

The dinner table is the best place for family conversation. Dinnertime means more than just consuming food and information. It is the perfect opportunity for the exchange of ideas and opinions. Family jokes and memories are forged around the dinner table. These are moments that belong only to your family. They are private times. You can say things at the dinner table that couldn't be shared outside the family. These conversations give your family a sense of identity and belonging.

The dinner table is the best place for family formation. How are family values passed from parents to children? It usually happens when you least expect it. . .in the unplanned moments. But it only happens when you are together and talking with each other. There is no better place for this to occur than at dinner time. Lectures in the living room can be ineffective, but conversations around the dinner table about character, morality, integrity, and behavior are much more palatable between bites of spaghetti. It is around your family's dinner table that each of you will discover a sense of identity—who you are with God, with your family, and with yourself.

Perhaps a family dinner time every evening is impossible in your household. If so, don't succumb to frustration and chop the dinner table into kindling for the fireplace. Infrequent use of the dinner table increases its significance.

Whether it is used several nights a week or less often, and regardless of how it is displayed, your dinner table can be significant in the life of your family. That's saying a lot for a piece of furniture.

...IN THE SMALL STUFF

* Even though the food may be the same, your family will receive more nourishment at the dinner table than at TV trays.

- The food *on* the table is not as important as the conversation *across* the table.

- Breakfast may be the most important *meal* of the day, but dinner can be the most important *time* of the day.

- A strong family usually has well-worn seat cushions at the dinner table.

- The best thing to serve at dinnertime is food for thought.

Beauty is all about us,
but how many people are blind to it!
People take little pleasure in
the natural and quiet and simple things of life.

Pablo Casals

NINE

HOUSE BEAUTIFUL

There are many ways to make your house beautiful, and most aren't expensive. Oh, you can pour over the home fashion magazines and dream about remodeling your kitchen with granite counters and a stainless steel gas stove. You can put in a pool or buy new furniture. All of these home improvements would certainly help to make your house more beautiful, but the stress you would incur from the cost could minimize your enjoyment.

There are other, more economical things you can do to beautify your home, and these won't keep you up at night. Fresh flowers, for example, bring vibrant color and a definite sense of style to both the outside and interior of your home. Artwork of any kind beautifies your home. And don't automatically assume that a gallery painting is your only option. Even discount stores carry some tasteful prints, and you never know what you'll find at a garage sale or flea market. Get things you enjoy, that express your taste and style.

And that's another thing. Beauty is more about style—your style—than it is about décor. Collect objects and furnishings that you and your family can enjoy because they reflect what your family is all about (this includes family pictures on the walls and the kids' artwork on the refrigerator). Someone should be able to walk into your home and connect the small touches with your family's personality.

Get your family involved in creating a personality for your home. This is where true beauty and meaning will shine through. What kind of statement does your family want to make? This isn't just for show, but to remind each of you daily that your home is more than a roof over your heads; it's a place that shows who you are and what you believe.

If God is in your family, then He should be in your home as well, through the music that fills your rooms, the books that line your shelves, and even the pictures that hang on your walls. Remember, it's the small stuff that makes the difference, whether it's in your life or in your home.

...In the Small Stuff

* Keep everything in your house in order:

    —Keep your bills paid.

    —Keep your beds made.

    —Keep your garden weeded.

    —Be available as needed.

* When people walk into your home, they should get a peaceful, easy feeling.

* Make your home a place where your family likes to gather.

* Make your home a place where friends like to drop by.

Cheerfully share your home with those
who need a meal or a place to stay.

1 Peter 4:9

TEN

HOSPITALITY

Hospitality is often defined as the display of thoughtfulness to strangers and guests. That is not too difficult. When you invite visitors into your home, whether they are new acquaintances or special friends, everyone in the family seems to be on "good behavior." Kindness and courtesy fill the air.

But having guests over for dinner is only part of hospitality—the easy part. The more challenging aspect of hospitality happens the moment the door shuts when the visitors leave. Now the real test of hospitality begins: Can your family treat each other with the same attention and respect that is reserved for special visitors?

Hospitality is so much more than serving tea and cookies in your home to the Ladies Missionary Guild, or offering your backyard for the company barbeque. It involves creating an environment within the home, and a mentality within your family, that treats everyone as a special guest. Your family members certainly deserve as much courtesy as a stranger receives in your home. Yet the natural tendency is to save our good behavior for the people we hardly know, while our family members are subjected to the less desirable aspects of our personality.

True hospitality creates an atmosphere where everyone, family and guests alike, feels special. It makes your home a place where visitors want to return and where your family feels comfortable. It makes your house the place where everyone wants to be. They won't be coming for the food and beverages (although you better keep both in ample supply); they will be at your house because it is a place where they feel appreciated.

This hospitality mentality doesn't happen automatically, and it won't become a habit if it is rehearsed only as often as the good china gets used. It has to be an attitude that everyone in the family adopts. It won't be easy. (Seeing each other in your pajamas seems to destroy the "special guest" illusion.) But with each kind gesture and display of courtesy, your home will become more like a place you would want to visit and stay for a while. That is what hospitality is all about.

...IN THE SMALL STUFF

- You know you have mastered the art of hospitality when its time for your children to leave home, but they don't want to go.

- The world is full of places to go, but your home should be the place where people want to stay.

- You know you have mastered the art of hospitality when people leave according to schedule with the impression that they could have stayed forever.

- In a hospitable home, everyone serves each other because they all feel special.

- You know you have mastered the art of hospitality when it means an inconvenience to you, but you don't consider it as one.

Music is for the soul what wind is for the ship,
blowing her onwards in the direction
in which she is steered.

William Booth

ELEVEN

MUSIC

"Music is a gift from God." You may agree with that statement, but it may or may not be true all the time, depending on where the music is coming from, how loud it is, and whether or not it's your style.

Music has the ability to inspire emotion. You can specifically remember where you were and who you were with the first time you heard certain songs. You can also get worked up when you hear other kinds of music you don't like, especially if one of your kids is listening to it.

Then there are those times when you hear a choir sing or bells chime or a soft song at a wedding that nearly makes you cry. Then you know that music is indeed God's gift. The trick is, how do you keep the music in your life on the level of a divine gift rather than a horrible sound?

Well, you can't control the music in public places, like the mall, a concert, or a teenager's car. You may not even be able to control the music coming from your own kid's room. But you can set the tone for the music in your family. This may seem like a small thing, but that's exactly why you need to get involved. Take charge, not in dictating what your kids should listen to (you've got bigger battles than that anyway), but by becoming the family deejay (that's disc jockey for the uninitiated) whenever your family is together for special occasions.

For starters, program the music for family meals (yes, they are special occasions), family car trips, and family holiday gatherings. Play music everyone can enjoy and even appreciate. And on certain occasions, like Sunday mornings, fill your home and your car with the glorious music of heaven, whether it's Bach, Handel, or contemporary praise and worship music. You will be amazed how God will fill your thoughts and emotions with His presence through the music.

Then perhaps you will agree that music is a gift from God.

...In the Small Stuff

- Study the life stories of composers like Bach and Handel and tell them to your family when you play their music.

- Read a book about the stories of famous hymns.

- Rather than criticizing the music your kids listen to, do your best to understand it.

- Ask your kids to give your music a try (unless you like Lawrence Welk).

- Make it a goal to listen to music more than you watch television.

And you must love the Lord your God with all your heart,
all your soul, and all your strength.
And you must commit yourselves wholeheartedly
to these commands I am giving you today.
Repeat them again and again to your children.
Talk about them when you are at home
and when you are away on a journey,
when you are lying down
and when you are getting up again.

Deuteronomy 6:5–7

THE SPIRITUAL FAMILY

TWELVE
GOD

What role should God have in your family? Should He be relegated to an insignificant influence, or should He have preeminence over all things? The correct answer is obvious, but sometimes the life we lead suggests that we have gotten our priorities mixed up.

Does your family talk about God in the context of your everyday circumstances? If His name is only mentioned as an expletive, then you should not be surprised if God seems nonexistent.

Does your family turn to God only in times of crisis or emergency? Certainly God is there in those times, but He may seem distant to you because your contact with Him is so sporadic.

Does you family treat God like a holy rabbit's foot. . .

looking to Him for good luck and protection? This concept of God might actually lead to a lack of faith in Him when your "luck" turns bad.

Or maybe your family interacts with God only as a religious ritual. It is as if you have Him in a box, and you bring Him out for display on Sundays and major religious holidays. The rest of the time, you keep Him in the box on a shelf in the closet, where He won't interfere with your daily activities. If this is your approach, your family must think of God as cold and impersonal.

God deserves a place in your family, and it is *first* place. And your family deserves to know God is real and personal. They need to know that He is vitally interested in the events of their lives. . .from the major events to the minor circumstances. But God won't intrude on you or your family. He is like a perfect gentleman, waiting to be invited as a guest into your lives.

Your family can experience the real and living God, but you must approach this relationship like others that you value. You can't expect to develop a close friendship with someone whom you totally ignore. You need to acknowledge God's presence, recognize His activity in your lives, and appreciate His provisions. Stated simply: You need to make room for God in your lives. When you do, you'll be amazed at the difference. You'll see God's hand directing you, you'll hear His voice comforting you, and you'll sense His spirit embracing you. He will be real to you.

Although God deserves to have priority in the lives of your family members, don't do it just for His sake. Put Him in first place for the sake of your family.

...IN THE SMALL STUFF

* We should give God the same place in our family that He holds in the universe.

* Let God have control in your family. He can do more with them than you can.

* Before God will do something *for* you, He usually wants to do something *in* you.

* If you only turn to God when you are in trouble, then you have to be worried about how He is going to get your attention.

* If you keep God *outside* of your family, there will be problems *inside* your family.

Your Father knows exactly what you need
even before you ask him!

Jesus, in Matthew 6:8

THIRTEEN
PRAYER

Most people would say they pray, and most would agree that prayer is effective. But how many of us would believe that prayer is a powerful way to bring our families closer to each other as well as closer to God?

When you were young, your parents told you to "say your prayers." You probably learned to say a prayer like, "Now I lay me down to sleep, I pray the Lord my soul to keep." Maybe your family had a certain prayer for meals, or you learned the Lord's Prayer in church. There's nothing wrong with saying those kinds of prayers. They help establish the habit of prayer.

But rather than simply memorizing prayers to recite at

meals, in church, and before bed, why not develop a family prayer time when everyone gets to participate? Take the initiative in this area by explaining to your family what prayer really is: talking to God. Prayer is thanking God for His involvement in the details of each of your lives. Of course, to discover what those details are, you have to talk to each other first. Before you pray as a family, share what God is doing in your life and ask other family members to do the same.

Prayer is also asking God to work in those areas where you feel vulnerable. In your family, those areas probably include school, work, and relationships. Maybe there are some small things in your family that need to be brought to God in prayer, things you should be dealing with. He's interested in all of them, and He longs to hear you talk to Him about them.

When you first talk as a family about the things you're going to pray about, you end up talking about important stuff. Small stuff and big stuff. Stuff that matters to others in the family. Stuff that matters to you.

The simple exercise of praying together regularly as a family will do more to strengthen your family than anything else you could do together.

...In the Small Stuff

- "The family that prays together stays together" is more than a nice saying; it's the truth.

- As your family grows closer to God in prayer, it will grow closer together.

- Prayer is the first thing you should do when a family crisis arises. It is also the second, third, and fourth thing you should do.

- Here's a proverb to teach your family: Pray like it depends on God and work like it depends on you.

- Prayer is a privilege. Don't take it for granted.

All Scripture is inspired by God
and is useful to teach us what is true
and to make us realize what is wrong in our lives.
It straightens us out and teaches us to do what is right.
It is God's way of preparing us in every way.

2 Timothy 3:16–17

FOURTEEN
THE BIBLE

We all like to get mail. We can't resist the urge to run outside the moment that we hear the letter carrier close the door on the mailbox. For all we know, only junk mail may be waiting for us. But it doesn't matter, because we are anxious to see if there is a message from a friend or something important and pertinent to our lives.

And our anticipation about unopened mail is equally evident with e-mail from the Internet. If you are computer literate, you know the thrill of clicking on the mailbox icon with expectant hope that you will hear the computer generated voice say: "You've got mail."

That same sense of excitement should overwhelm us as

we open God's Word, the Bible. After all, the Bible, in its truest sense, is a collection of letters that God has written directly to each of us. Penned by people who were inspired by God for each written word, the Bible is God's "mail" to us. His letters tell us everything that He wants us to know about Himself, and everything that we need to know about ourselves.

The Bible can be the divine guidebook for your family, but not if it is regarded as antiquated literature and dry history, fables and fairy tales. Your family needs to realize that the Bible is the very words of God that can equip you for life and for eternity. Nothing is more contemporary. Within its pages you can find the answers to the questions and issues that you struggle with each day: morality, integrity, relationships, finances, discouragement, love, life, and death.

Reading the Bible is not drudgery when you understand what you are reading. It should be part of the daily routine for each member of your family. Between the covers of that sacred book is the information God wants you to know each day. Personal information about you and for you, written by the One who knows you best.

Don't let a day go by without reading the personal and intimate message that God has written for you. As you look at your Bible on the shelf, hear the voice of God whisper: "You've got mail."

…In the Small Stuff

- Like many other books, the Bible tells you about its author. Unlike any other book, the Bible tells you about yourself.

- The Bible will find you where you are, and it will show you where you ought to go.

- A Bible that's read so often that it is falling apart is usually owned by a family that isn't.

- Your family won't acquire a taste for the Word of God if you only give them samples at Christmas and Easter.

- God can speak to you through the Bible, but you can't hear Him if you keep the cover closed.

He cannot have God for his father
who refuses to have the church for his mother.

St. Augustine

FIFTEEN
CHURCH

God loves families. After all, He designed the concept. In His plan, family units are the basic building blocks of society. God also used a "family" blueprint when He designed the church. But while a church may be composed of many individual families, God intends that all of the church members interact together as a single family. The similarities (and benefits) may surprise you.

An obvious similarity is the intergenerational composite of the family and the church. Just as your extended family may include infants and seniors, the members of the church span the age spectrum. Think of how this arrangement can benefit you if you regularly participate in a church.

Your church family can provide you with the exuberance of the young and the wisdom of the mature. Within this context of diversity you can appreciate qualities, experiences, and opinions of people with perspectives different than your own.

With a family, there is a sense of belonging. Your family ties give you a sense of identity and a sense of being connected to something larger than yourself. So it is with a church. Under the authority of the Heavenly Father, you can enjoy a brother and sister relationship with your "church family." You may be surprised to notice that you can grow as close to the members of your church family as to those in your biological family. In a church operating as God intended, you will have continual support and encouragement. You won't have to endure sickness or misfortune alone; some of your "brothers and sisters" will be by your side. You will want to share all of the events of your life, whether in celebration or sorrow, with your church family. They will be cheering you on in victory, and consoling you in defeat. And you will be doing the same for them. . .because that's what being a family is all about.

A family has a shared heritage, and so does the church. With the family, you can pull out the family photo album and see the common ancestors—the lineage that connects you. In the church, you won't have a photo album, but you do have a book that clearly identifies your common ancestry: the Bible. This doesn't mean you can trace your family tree back to Adam and Eve, but your shared belief in the God of the Bible connects you with each other. In this sense, the bonds of the church may be stronger than those of your biological family. After all, you didn't get to pick your biological ancestors, and you may have little in common with your relatives (at least you'll think so after the family reunion). But with the members of your church family, you are bonded by a common love of God and commitment to the Scripture.

God designed the family to function together in harmony: The husband honors his wife and serves her with sacrificial love like Christ displayed; the wife, in turn, responds with love for her husband; the children love and honor the parents; and the parents raise the children with responsibility and respect. The relationships in the "church family" are to operate the same way. No one is more important than anyone else; everyone has a role in contributing to the spiritual growth and encouragement of each other.

But we can't ignore the obvious. A variety of nuts grow on your family tree, and with some of them you would prefer to saw off their branch. And in your church you'll find a few oddballs, too. But this is no reason to stay away altogether. Remember that if the church only admitted people who didn't need it, you couldn't attend either. If a few people irritate you, view them as an opportunity to practice the godly virtues of patience and forgiveness *and love*.

Your personal family is not perfect, and your church family won't be either. But all the good aspects God intended for a family can by found in a church. That family is not complete without you, and you aren't complete without them. That's the way God designed it.

...IN THE SMALL STUFF

- Your biological family is for a lifetime; your church family is for eternity.

- Church is where you will meet family you never knew you had.

- You are never too bad to go to church, and you are never too good to stay away.

- You will have a better time in *your* house if your family spends time in *God's* house.

- With your relatives, the family resemblance is usually seen in the face. With your church, the family resemblance is usually seen in the heart.

God loves a cheerful giver.

2 Corinthians 9:7 (NIV)

SIXTEEN

STEWARDSHIP

There is a good barometer for telling how your family feels about God: money. Now, wait! Before you mistake us for those types on television that say God's blessings are in direct proportion to the amount of digits on your contribution check, let us explain. We aren't talking about *how much* you give. (We hear you breathing a sign of relief.) God is more interested in your *attitude* about giving than the *amount* of your giving. Your attitude about money reveals much about your relationship with God.

"Stewardship" is the way in which you handle what God has given to you. Of course, you want your family to be good stewards of the finances God has given to you. But stewardship means much more than throwing bucks in the offering plate, clipping newspaper coupons, or being a whiz with your Quicken computer program. While your charitable contributions and responsible budgeting are a part of it, there is much more to stewardship than that.

Stewardship involves perspective. Your family needs to realize that everything you have comes from God. Oh, sure, one or more of you actually brings home a paycheck, but God worked in the circumstances that provided the job.

Stewardship involves priorities. When does God get "paid"? Is He the last one? Are you giving to your church and the other ministries only after everything else has been purchased and paid for? Is God getting just the leftovers (if there are any)? God deserves first place in our lives. That means our finances, too. Giving a portion to God first reflects an attitude that God has priority in your family finances.

Stewardship is a privilege. Are you excited about giving to God? You should be. God doesn't really need our money, but our gifts can be an expression of our gratitude for His constant provision. Also, your gifts can be used in ministry to help others. When we understand what God has done for us, we will consider it a privilege to help others.

Your household probably isn't any different from most other families. The paycheck proceeds are in high demand.

Everybody wants a chunk, and there may not be enough to go around. But God isn't standing in line with His hand outstretched. He wants you to respond and come to Him on your own. Whether you are willing to put something in His hand reveals what is in your heart.

...In the Small Stuff

- What you *earn* affects the quality of your living; what you *give* affects the quality of your life.

- If you think you can't give when you have little, then you won't give when you have much.

- If you can't give generously, at least give what you deducted on your income tax return.

- We should give to God until it hurts—but Christ gave to us until He died.

- If you give generously to God, He won't be any richer, but you will be.

There is nothing which my heart desires more
than to see you, the members of this church,
distinguished for holiness.

Charles H. Spurgeon

The term *holy day* intimidates most people. Somehow we assume that a holy day is a sacred, solemn occasion where no one smiles because we figure holy days are all about God, and He certainly doesn't want us to be happy on these special days devoted to Him.

Well, there is some truth in that assumption. Holy days are *sacred* because they are dedicated to God (that's what *sacred* means). But they are far from solemn. In fact, at the heart of the meaning of *holy day* is the concept of *celebration* (that's where our word *holiday* comes from).

To the ancient Hebrews, a holy day was a time of joy and gladness to celebrate what God had done for them. Even now Jewish people observe holy days like Passover to remember God's care and deliverance. In your family, you may count special days like Easter and Christmas as holy days, and that's good. You may hold these days as sacred, which is also good, since they help you remember what God did for you by sending Jesus to earth.

We'd like for you to go one step further and consider these holy days as times of celebration. Another part of the meaning of holy day is a festival or feast, which is the reason why we traditionally prepare special meals at Easter or Christmas. In fact, the idea of eating together to celebrate the things God has done for us comes from the Bible. Jesus compared His relationship with us to "sharing a meal as friends" (Revelation 3:20). And heaven is described as a big wedding feast (Revelation 19:9).

When you sit down together with family and friends on special holy days like Easter and Christmas, and special holidays like Thanksgiving, don't just focus on the food. Give your attention to God, your Provider and Deliverer. Teach your family on these special occasions to give praise to God for His careful and loving involvement in your lives.

Encourage each person gathered around your table to talk about God in personal terms. Offer a thoughtful prayer of thanksgiving for His goodness, and pray for those who are experiencing personal difficulties, illness, or family strife. Pray for those in other parts of the world who are repressed and persecuted.

Besides the obvious holy days we've already mentioned, which each come up once a year, you may want to consider celebrating another often overlooked holy day that occurs once a week. We're talking, of course, about the Sabbath.

In the Old Testament, the Sabbath simply referred to the seventh day of the week. This was an important observance, because "God blessed the seventh day and declared it holy, because it was the day when he rested from his work of creation" (Genesis 2:3). God considered the Sabbath so important that He included it in the Ten Commandments: "Remember to observe the Sabbath by keeping it holy. Six days a week are set apart for your daily duties and regular work, but the seventh day is a day of rest dedicated to the Lord your God" (Exodus 20:8-10).

Most of us observe the Sabbath on Sunday, but that doesn't change the commandment. As God's people, we are to set one day a week aside by *resting* from our routine and work. Unfortunately, most of us are just as busy on Sundays—maybe more so—as we are during the week. We rush to go places and get things done.

May we suggest a new approach—God's approach—to the Sabbath? Whether you observe the seventh day on Saturday or Sunday, set it apart for God. Celebrate His involvement in the big stuff in our world and the small stuff in your family. Going to church is a great way to do this, but don't just leave it to your minister or priest to celebrate for you. Continue to rest in God at home by sharing a meal as a family and talking about what God is doing in your lives.

...IN THE SMALL STUFF

* A rested mind stays sharp; a lazy mind gets dull.

* Thank God for His blessings every day, but do it publicly once a week.

* Even God took a day off. What makes you think you don't have to?

* Resting in God leads to refreshment in life.

W hen the bread is broken and
the wine is poured into the cup at the Eucharist,
we are brought face to face with our own need
for evangelism, with our own need for brokenness
and the call for our lives to be outpoured. . . .

Erice Fairbrother

EIGHTEEN
SACRAMENTS

There are some terms of the Christian faith we hold dear that aren't found in the Bible. The word *Trinity*, describing the three-in-one nature of God the Father, God the Son, and God the Holy Spirit, isn't in the Bible, although the concept clearly is (check out Matthew 3:16-17). The same goes for the *rapture*, the future event when all Christians, dead and alive, will meet Jesus in the air. You won't find the actual word in the Bible, but there's no denying what it describes (see 1 Thessalonians 4:16-18).

Sacrament is another precious word we hold in high regard that isn't in the Bible. A sacrament is defined as a sign or a seal. The Latin root word for sacrament is a military term describing an oath of enlistment or a pledge. If you combine those two meanings, you capture the two aspects of sacraments: the promises of God to us and our pledge of dedication to God.

Within the Christian church, there are seven sacraments, including baptism, confirmation, the Eucharist (communion), and marriage. Depending on your church affiliation, you may observe some or all of the sacraments.

Where you family is concerned, if you attend church, you probably participate in communion on a regular basis. Also known as the Lord's Supper, this practice was initiated by Jesus Himself with His disciples the night before He was arrested and crucified (Luke 22:7-20). As they were eating supper, Jesus blessed a loaf of bread and broke it into pieces, which He gave to His disciples. The bread represented His body, about to be broken for them.

Then Jesus took a cup of wine and thanked God before giving it to His disciples. This represented His blood, shed for the forgiveness of sins. After offering the bread and the wine, Jesus said, "Do this in remembrance of Me," which is what the church has been doing ever since with the sacrament of communion.

Whereas communion is a sacrament we observe over and over, baptism usually occurs only once. The sacrament of baptism also comes from the example of Jesus, who was baptized by John the Baptist. For Jesus, baptism was a sign of approval and acceptance by God. It's the same for us when we're baptized, but it carries the additional meaning of repentance, or a change of direction. It means we say good-bye to the old life we had before entering into new life with God through Christ. The water suggests the washing away of sin.

These are lofty concepts because they are so important. Where your family is concerned, they are details you should not overlook. Don't enter into these and other sacraments lightly. Talk to your minister and pray together about getting your family involved. Study the sacraments in the Bible and read a book or two that will help explain them. God will show you in small ways how you should proceed, and He will bless your family if you do.

...IN THE SMALL STUFF

- There is a reason we usually practice the sacraments in church. God designed it that way.

- A personal relationship with God through Christ is crucial to fully understanding the sacraments.

- Each sacrament involves dedicating yourself to God.

- When you're dedicated to God, you are less likely to be distracted from doing what is right.

Laughter and weeping are the two
intensest forms of human emotion,
and these profound wells
of human emotion are to be
consecrated to God.

Oswald Chambers

FAMILY FUN

NINETEEN

HUMOR

We know that you are willing to do whatever it takes to strengthen your family. Whether it is time or energy or money, nothing would be too great a price if you could be assured that the family relationships would be improved. Well, we can't give you any guarantees, but we do have a suggestion that has a proven track record and a low cost.

We believe that a sense of humor can be a secret formula for success in your family. Laughter softens the rough edges in the relationships between family members. When your family is laughing together, all of the barriers that might separate them seem to disappear.

- The "hard feelings" over a past disagreement dissipate with laughter. Somehow the argument won't seem so important after a few mutual chuckles.

- Parents can't take themselves too seriously when they have a sense of humor about their idiosyncrasies and weaknesses. Your children will appreciate the fact that you are open and honest about your faults. (These flaws are painfully obvious to your children, so you might as well laugh about them. And your children will appreciate the fact that you aren't hypocritical and pretending to be perfect.)

- Your children will have an improved self-image if they can laugh about themselves. They will realize that it is okay to be less than perfect. They will learn to accept and appreciate their own uniqueness. With a healthy attitude about their own peculiarities, they will have a strong defense against peer pressure.

- You don't have to be a stand-up comic to pull this off. All it takes is a light-hearted spirit. A lively attitude. Playful teasing. A few practical jokes. Just make an effort, and you'll find that humor and laughter have a momentum that builds as others join in.

We suppose it is every parent's dream that their children will have fond memories of life at home. It is difficult to predict what memories they will carry with them in the future, but there is a way that you can monitor their impression of how things are going in your home right now. Look at their faces. Do you see grins or grimaces?

...In the Small Stuff

- A sense of humor is a sign of sanity.

- Laughter is the best medicine, even if you aren't sick.

- A sense of humor is like a repair kit. It can fix all sorts of problems.

- A sense of humor is like a survival kit. It can help you survive through all sorts of disasters.

- There is no loneliness in a home filled with laughter.

Take delight in the Lord,
and he will give you your heart's desires.

Psalm 37:4

TWENTY

RECREATION

As families we tend to take ourselves way too seriously. It goes something like this:

When you first decide to start a family, you worry about finances, you wonder if you'll have enough space in your house or apartment, and you suddenly get nervous about world conditions in general.

Then as your children get older, your attention shifts to them. How come they won't listen, why are they having trouble in school, how are you ever going to afford college, and why is car insurance so expensive? Through it all you do your best to keep the household going while balancing everyone's relationships.

Okay, so managing a family *is* serious business. That doesn't mean that *you* have to be serious, too. Refuse to succumb to your naturally negative tendencies. Rise above the rigor—if not the responsibility—of running your household and have some fun. Accent your routine with some family recreation.

When you recreate, you literally "create anew." Recreation involves diverting yourself from the everyday and the mundane for the purpose of revitalizing your interest in life, in each other, and in God. Or as a friend of ours puts it, "recreation is how you recharge your batteries."

Recreation doesn't have to be expensive. Too many of us think we have to spend a lot of money on fancy sports equipment or elaborate vacations in order to have fun. Wrong thinking! Enjoy the natural world that God created for us in the first place. God is delighted when we enjoy His created things: lakes, forests, the mountains, the ocean, the countryside—just about anything you can think of outdoors. God made it all, and to Him every detail is "excellent in every way" (Genesis 1:31).

Even the man-made gardens, golf courses, and water parks we enjoy as recreation ultimately come from God's creation. (What would they be without flowers, grass, and water?) So go ahead. Treat your family to some of the simple pleasures of life and feel renewed in the process.

…IN THE SMALL STUFF

- It's okay—and even admirable—to relax alone from time to time, as long as you do things with your family as well.

- There are two kinds of recreation: planned and spontaneous. Make time for both.

- When it comes to recreation, the best things in life are usually free (or at least relatively cheap).

- Don't take your recreation—whatever it is—too seriously. (If you do, you probably play golf.)

- It's okay to be good at the things you enjoy doing outdoors. Just don't try to be perfect.

Wherever you go,
God is there.

TWENTY-ONE

TRAVEL

We are big proponents of family travel. Getting out of the house and into a different environment can have many benefits for your family. Together you can experience new adventures. Together you can meet new people and see new sights. In these different situations, the foreign circumstances will bond your family together.

A trip to a foreign country can be a particularly enlightening and cohesive experience for your family. But don't think that you have to postpone family travel until you have saved the price of a new house to stay a week in Paris. Your family travel doesn't have to be that extravagant.

One particular family travel event can be inexpensive—

and it is guaranteed to give you the greatest opportunity to create memories and see God's provision all at the same time: the family car trip. An adventure of this sort is not for the faint of heart, but look what awaits you:

- You will learn patience as you answer the repeated plea for the "ETA" (estimated time of arrival—which is the contemporary version of "Are we there yet?").

- You will learn dependence upon God's provision as you find your way after being lost.

- You will learn to trust God for protection as you are changing the flat tire on the shoulder of the interstate.

- And perhaps most important of all, you will be learning these lessons together as a family (if you are bold enough to admit to your kids that you are lost). These are excellent opportunities to teach your children about God being in the middle of your circumstances.

Some of the memories from car trips will last forever. Oh, your kids may forget about the side trip to see "The

World's Largest Ball of Twine" or the "Petrified Mushroom Garden," but they will remember laughing at each other's antics, singing together, and playing car games to pass the time. And after all, isn't that what family outings are all about?

So, whether it is a chateau in Southern France, or the Motel Six in Fresno, include family travel on your agenda. Even a weekend journey can be a trip that lasts a lifetime in the memory of your family.

...IN THE SMALL STUFF

- Sometimes you strengthen your home when all of you get away from it together.

- You have to go away to learn that there is no place like home.

- The family that travels together experiences God together.

- Even if you forget the camera, scenes of your family trip will be captured in the mind of your child.

Above all, guard your heart,
for it affects everything you do.

Proverbs 4:23

TWENTY-TWO
ENTERTAINMENT

We live in a culture that loves amusement. We love visiting Disney World, Las Vegas, Universal Studios, and even the state fair, as long as we get bright lights and plenty of action.

We love our cable TV that offers an endless variety of sitcoms, sports channels, political commentary, and news. We can't seem to get enough of the movies and movie stars, either. Just when you thought videos (we love them, too) would keep people snuggled up at home, Hollywood is more popular than ever. Then there's that relatively recent home commodity, the personal computer (or iMac for all you Apple lovers), with its virtual window to millions of Web sites, games, and chat rooms.

No matter how you twist and turn it, no matter how many variations you come up with, all of these forms of amusement and entertainment exist because we humans can't seem to get enough.

Some people view all of this amusement as nothing more than a giant manure pile (sorry to be so graphic, but you've got to admit, the description isn't that far off). Others see it as a grand opportunity to expand our horizons and become people who better understand the world and ourselves.

Like us, your view of the vast entertainment machine is probably somewhere in between. You enjoy being amused as much as the next person, but you've got your limits, and besides, you have a family to look after. You think that no one in their right mind would have an "anything goes" attitude when it comes to the kind and the quantity of entertainment you allow in your home—or outside the home for that matter. And you would be correct.

When it comes to the overwhelming stream of information and entertainment (increasingly called *infotainment*) available 24 hours a day to you and your family, someone has to be the "gatekeeper." Someone has to screen out the toxic waste and regulate the flow of everything else.

Actually, we are all responsible for guarding what comes into our lives through our five senses: our sight, hearing, touch, smell, and taste. These are the gates through which all forms of amusement and entertainment must ultimately pass. Our senses are, in fact, the gates to our very beings, which include our physical, emotional, and spiritual dimensions.

The Bible pretty much condenses these senses into one main gate—the heart. When you think about it, that makes a lot of sense (no pun intended). The heart is the most important organ in your body. It pumps the blood of life so you can live. So when the wisest man who ever lived made this statement, he knew what he was talking about:

"Above all else, guard your heart, for it affects everything you do."

Everything you let in through your heart's gate affects who you are and what you do. If you are a spiritually maturing person, you will post a guard that says, "Stop! Who goes there?" to the infotainment knocking relentlessly at your heart's door. If that part of your life isn't important to you—or you don't know any better—then your heart is like a Denny's restaurant: *always open.*

As the family gatekeeper, you are not only responsible for your own heart, but for the hearts of others as well. You can and you should help the children in your family make decisions about their entertainment. We would suggest, however, that you make it your goal to help them develop their own discernment muscles, so that when you're not around to help them make wise decisions, they will be able to do the right thing on their own.

We're not talking about tolerance for certain forms of entertainment, but rather wisdom in all things. Keep in mind that there are a lot of good things that come knocking at the gate. You want your children and others in your family to open their heart's door at the appropriate time so they don't miss out on the blessings both big and small that God wants to bring to their lives.

Right living starts with right thinking, which is another way to look at wisdom. That's why the Bible says: "Fix your thoughts on what is true and honorable and right. Think about things that are pure and lovely and admirable. Think about things that are excellent and worthy of praise" (Philippians 4:8).

...In the Small Stuff

- As a gatekeeper, you can never let your guard down.

- It would be nice if the people who produce the entertainment you enjoy shared your values, but they don't.

- There's room in the world for talented people who want to create entertainment that glorifies God.

To keep your marriage brimming,
With love in the loving cup,
Whenever you're wrong, admit it,
Whenever you're right, shut up.

Ogden Nash

FAMILY RELATIONSHIPS

TWENTY-THREE

MARRIAGE

Marriage seems to be the favorite topic of comedians. Everyone laughs at the descriptions of a husband who is either snoozing in the recliner, belching and scratching, or driving around lost but refusing to ask for directions. And the stereotypes of the wife aren't much better. She is usually described as a nag, a shopaholic, or a neat freak. But the disrespect of most spouses for each other is no laughing matter. Let's face it. Most married people believe that a spouse is like arthritis: a bit of a pain, but you learn to live with it.

Marriage doesn't have to be that way, because God didn't design it that way. In God's plan, marriage is a lifetime union between a husband and wife, a union that completes each of them. Together they are a whole. They complement each other and bring to the relationship exactly what the other needs.

Instead of laughing at your spouse, or focusing on those habits that irritate you so much, try looking at your spouse from God's perspective. God specifically and uniquely designed your spouse *for you.* The Master Designer knew the kind of person you would need to smooth out your own rough spots. So look for the strengths in your spouse that off-set your weaknesses. Instead of tuning out what your spouse says, consider that those words may be exactly what God wants you to hear.

This new perspective won't come easily. After all, you have probably spent most of your marriage (beginning shortly after the honeymoon) trying to change your spouse. It may take some time to reprogram your own thinking to recognize that God may be using your spouse to change *you.*

And there's more, too. Just as God is using your spouse to work in *your* life, you are God's most obvious method of ministering in your *spouse's* life. If God wants your spouse to be comforted or encouraged or consoled, who is He most likely to use for that purpose? You! Quit the ridiculing and complaining that seems to come so naturally. God wouldn't talk to your spouse like that, and He doesn't want you to do so either. Talk to your spouse like God would. (Don't feel obligated to use those fancy "thee's" and "thou's." God doesn't speak in King James English any more.) Remember that God wants to use you in your marriage to spiritually and emotionally support your spouse.

Think about the transformation that can occur in your marriage if you both attempt to be God's servant to each other. No longer will your marriage be characterized by vicious sarcasm or ridicule. Instead, each of you will be looking for opportunities to help the other. And if you welcome your spouse's input as being helpful instead of hurtful, you will stop being defensive with each other.

How sad that many marriages are tolerated instead of celebrated. But what else can we expect when the relationship is like a battlefield? By appreciating what God wants to accomplish in your life through your spouse—and by understanding the role you play in God's effort to minister to your spouse—your marriage will become a sanctuary. It will be a place to which you both retreat for mutual protection, care, and comfort. You will feel safe in your marriage because the relationship will be free from character assassination. In a hectic and hostile world, your marriage will be your place of refuge.

Try to see yourself and your spouse from God's perspective. It will change the way that you live. It will change the way you love. And that is no laughing matter.

...IN THE SMALL STUFF

* You can contribute more to your marriage with an open mind than an open mouth.

* Before marriage, you should concentrate on *finding* the right person. After marriage, you should concentrate on *being* the right person.

* Show at least the same courtesy to your spouse that you show to strangers.

- With the faults and failings of your spouse, have a thick skin and a short memory.

- If you approach marriage as a 50/50 proposition, you'll only have half a life.

Babies have the unique ability
to make you feel old
while keeping you young.

TWENTY-FOUR
BABIES

Babies can either be a source of amazing joy or unending annoyance, depending on your perspective and circumstances. If the baby is yours, and it's new, and it's your first, there is no greater joy. On the other hand, if you're on an airplane and you want to take a nap and there's an oversized baby with a runny nose and sticky hands screaming next to you because his diaper is full and you're in rough weather so his mother can't change him right now, well, there is no greater annoyance.

It's not the baby's fault, of course. Babies aren't deliberately annoying; screaming and smelling is just what they do, especially when we try to put them in non-baby situations.

Babies aren't deliberately joyful, either. They can't help being cute, cuddly, and charming. It's what they do.

When it comes to your family, babies take on special significance. Upon their arrival, they automatically become the absolute center of attention. The responsibility of caring for and feeding a newborn infant may fall quite naturally to Mother, but in a family everyone needs to gets involved in giving a baby what it needs most—loving attention.

In this era of elaborate devices designed to hold and carry a baby, the very human touch of a mother and father and siblings and grandparents and aunts and uncles and cousins becomes a necessity. In the old days (when you grew up) parents carried their babies everywhere. Now we transport them.

Likewise, when so many babies are necessarily relegated to day care centers or non-family caretakers for hours at a time, the importance of a baby playing, learning, laughing, and crying with his or her own family for hours at a time becomes enormous.

Babies don't become physically healthy, emotionally balanced, spiritually sensitive, and personally enjoyable little people on their own. It takes a family to attend to the small stuff in a baby's life. It takes a family to introduce that little person to God and His goodness. And it takes a family to teach that little one that God not only cares, but also wants to get involved in the details of his or her life.

...IN THE SMALL STUFF

- Changing a diaper puts you in touch with the basics of life.

- Smile whenever you see a baby.

- Hold your baby as often as possible.

- Read to your baby whenever you can.

- Love your baby always.

Don't let anyone think less of you
because you are young.

1 Timothy 4:12

TWENTY-FIVE
TEENAGERS

The teen years are difficult. For both the kids and the parents. Teenagers are at an awkward stage:

- They aren't yet adults, but they think they are.
- They have outgrown being little kids, but at times they still act like them.
- They want to be independent, but they want their parents to pay for everything.

Part of the difficulty of living with teenagers is their failure to live up to the parents' expectations. You might assume that this is the fault of the teenagers. Well, maybe. But perhaps a share of the blame can be placed on the parents for having *unrealistic* expectations. Now, don't get us wrong. We aren't parent-bashing here. (After all, we have been parents for a lot longer than we were teenagers.) We just know that when you're under the pressure of being a parent, it is easy to forget that teenagers are still behaviorally schizophrenic—sometimes they act like adults and sometimes they don't.

Parents often make the mistake of remembering the fleeting times when their teenager showed responsibility and maturity, and then the parents use that behavior as the standard. But the teenagers won't always measure up to that benchmark because their maturity isn't consistent yet. Teenagers have "transitory maturity." It comes and goes. (Hopefully, over time, the maturity will stay a little longer each time it comes.)

It might be helpful if you discuss your expectations with your teenagers. We suggest expectations that are based on the evolutionary stage your teenager is going through. We don't mean that your teenager is a Neanderthal (although there are times. . .). We just know that it is unrealistic to expect constant perfection (because parents can't even reach *that* goal). Here are a few examples (and we expect that your teenager will like the odd numbered ones, and you'll appreciate the even numbered ones).

Expectation #1: *Expect your teenagers to make mistakes.* They will be able to live up to this expectation. In fact, they may be over-achievers on this one. But if your expectations include mistakes from your teenager, then you won't be surprised when they happen. Oh, you may still get disappointed, but perhaps you won't pop a cranial corpuscle. Make sure that your teenagers know that Expectation #1 does not entitle them to make mistakes intentionally. It is reserved for mistakes that they make out of ignorance, immaturity, or sheer stupidity. It doesn't cover goofing up on purpose. (See Expectation #2.)

Expectation #2: *Expect your teenagers to learn from their mistakes.* This is an important corollary to Expectation #1, and it recognizes the transition of teenagers from childhood to adulthood. Making honest mistakes is part of being a kid; learning from mistakes is a part of being an adult.

Expectation #3: *Expect that your teenagers won't tell you everything.* As part of the journey to independence, your teenager will want more privacy. (Crawling into the clothes hamper with the cordless phone is a clue.) Your curious inquiries will be viewed as cruel interrogations. Learn to be satisfied with monosyllabic responses.

Expectation #4: *Expect that you will be informed about the "who, what, where, and when" away from home.* Expectation #3 is an accommodation to the teenager's desire for privacy. Expectation #4 reflects the parent's duty to protect, teach, and advise their children. (If your teenagers scoff at the need for such supervision, remind them about Expectation #1.) So, given your parental responsibilities, it is reasonable to expect that you will know "where, when, what, and who" whenever your teenager isn't at home.

Expectation #5: *Expect that you won't be your teenager's best friend.* As much as you think that you are "cool" and "with it," your teenager thinks that you are old and outdated. (The fact that we use lingo like "cool" and "with it" proves that we are of a bygone era.) So, your teenager probably won't want to hang out with you at the mall. (And if you have to go there together, don't be surprised if you are ignored. . .or called by your first name instead of "Mom" or "Dad.")

Expectation #6: *Expect to be treated with respect.* Your teenager doesn't have to treat you like a best friend, but you at least deserve to be treated like a fellow human being. Common courtesy should not be abandoned just because you are related.

If these work for your family, please let us know. Unfortunately, we didn't think of them until after our kids had outgrown their teen years. Our children aren't the only ones who are smarter now than they used to be. So are we.

...IN THE SMALL STUFF

* Treat your teenagers like adults, but don't expect them to act that way.

* Try to understand your teenagers by listening to what they say.

* Your teenager hasn't had enough time to outgrow all the faults that you used to have.

* Teenagers think that they know all the answers, but they haven't heard all the questions.

* No one is as smart as teenagers think they are, and no one is as dumb as teenagers think their parents are.

Call it a clan, call it a network,
call it a tribe, call it a family.
Whatever you call it, whoever you are,
you need [your siblings].

Jane Howard

TWENTY-SIX
BROTHERS AND SISTERS

If God created families to nurture us, then He designed brothers and sisters to protect us. Brothers and sisters look out for each other, and not just in physical ways. Sure, you may have had a big brother or sister who stood up for you when the school bully took your milk money. But it's more likely that a sibling has given you emotional support and protection more often than you can count, and you have probably done the same for your own brother or sister.

That's why brothers and sisters can call each other at any time for any reason and get right down to the issues at hand. It doesn't matter how trivial the subject or how monumental the problem. Brothers and sisters understand each other. They know how to encourage, cajole, reprimand, and promote each other with complete honesty and with unconditional love.

Okay, maybe we're painting an idealistic picture here. After all, brothers and sisters fight and feud and sometimes go for long periods without communicating. Family business, politics, and even church matters have been know to drive siblings apart. Like a wood sliver under your skin, small irritations can fester and erupt into bigger sores that eventually overshadow the original issue.

That's the time to remember why God put you together with siblings in the first place, so you could share burdens, challenges, and victories—great and small. You have a special bond because you are people linked by a common heritage, and you are people forging a common legacy.

Whenever you're together with your siblings, reminisce about the small stuff you shared when you were younger. Talk about the ways God was there, even when you didn't realize it at the time. Then, plan how you can use your strengths as brothers and sisters to create a better world for your children, your nieces and nephews, and your parents. Pray for them and invite God into the details of all your lives.

...IN THE SMALL STUFF

- Tell your brothers and sisters how much you love and appreciate them. Call them if you have to.

- Anticipate your siblings' needs and offer to help.

- Adopted children are siblings, too, of course. Love them like your own flesh and blood.

- As a Christian, you share a common bond with your fellow brothers and sisters in Christ: You are all adopted into God's family.

- Call your siblings on their birthdays.

- Rejoice with your brothers and sisters when they succeed.

"Grandma, do you remember what it is like
to be a little girl like me?"
"Of course, darling."
"Grandma, do you remember what it's like
to get candy for no reason?"

TWENTY-SEVEN
GRANDPARENTS AND GRANDCHILDREN

You wouldn't try to sit on a milking stool that only had two legs. That would be foolish (unless you're a lawyer looking to sue the dairy farmer). A two-legged stool has no stability. It needs the third leg for balance and strength.

The same is true for families. No, they don't need a third leg. But they do need a third generation. There needs to be a relationship between grandparents and grandchildren. That third generation brings stability, balance, and strength to the family.

Grandparents bring a sense of history and heritage to the family. They can testify to God's continual provision through the years. Their lives tell the story of how God works in the details and circumstances of day-to-day events. Look for opportunities for your parents to tell their personal stories to your children (and your kids may be particularly interested in hearing tales about your behavior as a child).

With you, your kids will only be children. With your parents around, your kids will have the opportunity to be grandchildren. No child should ever miss the privilege of being a grandchild. Grandchildren get preferred status. A child gets disciplined, but a grandchild gets spoiled. There are rules for a child, but a grandchild has no limits. Grandparents will give your child the opportunity to be loved without demands or expectations. Include grandparents in family activities as often as possible, but also arrange for your children to spend time alone with their grandparents.

Don't despair if death or distance has robbed your family of that "third generation." There are many "grandparents" who are waiting to be adopted. You can find them in your neighborhood or in your church. The adoption process is easy. (It can get started at the dinner table or with a trip to the zoo.)

Grandparents can give your children a sense of acceptance. Grandchildren can do the same thing for your parents.

You'll get the benefit from both ends of the generational spectrum.

...In the Small Stuff

* Maybe the grandchildren wouldn't get so spoiled if you could spank the grandparents.

* A mom's life is hectic, but a grandmother can move at a child's pace.

* Your child may be average in many ways, but not in the eyes of your parents. Grandparents are the grandchild's greatest cheerleaders.

* Grandparents make great baby-sitters. They watch the grandchildren instead of the television.

* Time with grandparents is a vacation from reality.

From the loving example of one family
a whole state becomes loving.

Ancient proverb

TWENTY-EIGHT

UNCLES AND AUNTS

There's a wonderful adventure story in the Bible that concerns an uncle and his nephew. The uncle is Abraham, the father of the Hebrew nation, God's chosen people. Abraham's nephew is Lot, a brash, wayward young man whose greed overshadows his common sense.

As the story is told in Genesis 14, Lot and his family and all of his possessions have been captured by invaders. When Abraham hears about it, he assembles a group of loyal men from his own household and stages a surprise attack, rescuing Lot and his family while recovering all of his possessions in the process. Now there's an uncle! Someone who would risk his life and go into battle to rescue a helpless—if not completely innocent—nephew.

Those kind of dramatic rescue opportunities don't come up much these days, but there may be a time when you are called upon as an uncle or aunt to help out a nephew or a niece in trouble or in need. It may be a small thing, like providing transportation or a place to live, or it may require you to give of your resources or put your own reputation on the line.

The question is, can your brothers or sisters depend on you to help their kids when you're the only one who can? No doubt you had a favorite uncle or aunt growing up, and there may have been times when it was easier to talk to him or her than your own parents. Sometimes it just works that way, and it has nothing to do with who loves you more or who you love more. It's all about the right person being there for you at the right time.

Think about the ways God wants to use you in the lives of your nieces and nephews, or your uncles and aunts for that matter. Don't neglect your duty to pray for their health and well being. Let them know you're willing to help them no matter what the circumstances are. That way, if the opportunity to help comes up, you won't hesitate.

...IN THE SMALL STUFF

- Treat your nieces and nephews in the same way you would want your kids to be treated.

- When you love and respect your nieces and nephews, you do the same for their parents.

- Keep in touch with your aunts and uncles.

- Ask your uncles and aunts to tell you stories about your parents. You'll be surprised how much you learn about yourself.

- Make sure your nieces and nephews know they can come to you for help at any time.

W hether or not you enjoy your
family reunion is entirely up to you.
It's all relative.

TWENTY-NINE

FAMILY REUNIONS

At the appointed time, they begin to arrive. It is a strange assortment of humanity: Some appear to have lived under rocks, or traveled with the carnival sideshow, or escaped recently from the penitentiary for the criminally insane. From all directions, they converge on your home.

Is this a scene from the latest Stephen King made-for-television thriller? No, it's the family reunion!

Fear grips you as you open the door and begin to greet this bizarre assortment of cousins, and the in-laws of the cousins, and the friends of the children of the. . .hey, who are those kids, anyway? As you watch with helpless terror while your home is soiled and stained, you are comforted by your previous decision to defer recarpeting until after this fiasco. As you see your personal effects being fondled and sat upon, you find solace in your earlier precautionary measures of hiding everything that could be broken (or stolen).

Finally, the event is over. Like a frightened squirrel, you huddle on the couch to enjoy the silence of your own thoughts. Although you dare not speak these thoughts audibly, you come to the obvious conclusion that you are the only normal one in the entire family tree. (Unbeknownst to you, everyone else is thinking exactly the same thing about themselves as they leave your home.)

The scene we have just described was exaggerated (sort of). While we may feel some apprehension about family gatherings, they are never as bad as we dread. In fact, such periodic reunions can strengthen your family spiritually and emotionally. You will find that they can be very rewarding if you remember that God invented the family and has put you in one for a reason.

Family reunions also allow you to appreciate the diversity within your family tree. Enjoy the variety of personalities and perspectives. Value each relative for the differences he or she brings to your group.

Although each family member is a distinct and unique person, you shouldn't forget to appreciate the common bonds of ancestry that you share. In a time and society when people are lonely and detached, you will gain a real sense of belonging when your extended family meets together. Through your ancestors you can trace your nationality and ethnic roots. It probably only takes a few generations to trace your heritage to some other continent.

Your spiritual heritage, just like your family heritage, also may be graphically depicted by each life represented in the group. One ancestor may be responsible for bringing a godly influence and sensitivity to your family. If so, you can thank God for that person. Or you may realize that you are the one God has chosen to bring a spiritual influence to your family.

When the family reunion is all over, you might find yourself laughing about Uncle Harold's peculiarities. When the chuckling has subsided, don't forget to thank God for the beautiful, diverse gift of your family lineage.

- Don't complain about the relatives you are stuck with. Remember that they didn't get to make a choice about you either.

- Distant relatives don't have to stay that way.

- Geographic separation is no excuse for not staying in touch.

- Make every effort to respect the laws—even the in-laws.

The godly are concerned for
the welfare of their animals.

Proverbs 12:10

THIRTY

FAMILY PETS

"All dogs go to heaven." At least that's what a lot of us believe. Dogs have such good hearts, even if they do lick a lot. If we take care of them, they are loyal, forgiving, and nonjudgmental. They love us for who we are (so what if it's because we feed them). We love our family dogs because we see qualities in them we wished we saw in ourselves (except for the licking). Although cats don't possess many qualities we personally admire (unless you consider sleepiness and a general disinterest in humans as admirable), we don't mind having them around the house, and some people even like them as pets.

If you had a family pet when you were growing up, you

probably have one now. And if you have kids in the house, then you know that in addition to providing companionship and affection, a pet can be a source of instruction, especially for children.

The most obvious lesson we can learn from our pets is responsibility. Someone has to feed the dog, someone has to clean up after the dog, someone has to exercise the dog. These are small, simple details that need to be repeated every day. It's called caring and feeding. If we don't do it, nobody will. Our pets are totally dependent upon us for their welfare and well-being.

When you take this care and feeding business to a deeper level, it isn't that much of a stretch to compare the way we provide for our pets to the way God provides for us. Having said that, we don't want to give you the idea that we human beings are God's little pets. He didn't create us for His amusement, and He doesn't expect us to do little tricks or roll over so He can scratch our bellies. In fact, God created us in His image, so there is a likeness between God and us.

We're thinking about this comparison with pets more on the level of care and feeding. Just as our pets are totally dependent on us for their existence, we are completely dependent on God for all that we are and all that we have. Jesus addressed this care and feeding issue when He said, "So don't worry about having enough food or drink or clothing. . . . Your heavenly Father already knows all your needs, and he will give you all you need from day to day if you live for him and make the Kingdom of God your primary concern" (Matthew 6:31-33).

The more we view God as a provider—and teach our children to do the same—the more we will see that nothing is too small for His involvement. We will stop taking for granted our daily provisions and the small pleasures our family enjoys, and begin to see them all as coming from God.

Who knows? If we really begin to appreciate what God does for us, we may begin to develop the same kind of unconditional loyalty and affection for God that our family pet has for us, only with the true understanding that God is our creator and provider. He loves us more than anyone else ever could, and He has our best interests in mind at all times.

...In the Small Stuff

- Caring for your pet means more than feeding.

- Read a book about your pet's breed. If you don't know the breed of your pet, read about your pet's species. If you don't know the species, get a new pet.

- Remember that pets need exercise, whether you have a terrier or a hamster.

- God created animals for our benefit and enjoyment, not our cruelty and amusement.

- Children who learn to properly care for family pets learn valuable lessons about life.

For many people the heavy responsibilities of home
and family and earning a living absorb
all their time and strength.
Yet such a home—where love is—
may be a light shining in a dark place,
a silent witness to the reality and the love of God.

Olive Wyon

THIRTY-ONE

WORKING PARENTS

It's nearly become a fact of family life that both parents work. And if yours is a single-parent household, it's a virtual certainty that mom or dad (either of which could be you) works full-time.

Sometimes work can be very fulfilling. Other times it's a necessity and little more. Often it's difficult to balance the pressures of work with the demands of running a household and raising a family. We think, "If I keep this schedule up, something's going to suffer." But it doesn't have to be that way.

You may not be able to change your working situation, and we're not saying you should. We're not going to tell you that your family will deteriorate if you work, unless work has become the central focus of your life. What we'd like to suggest is that you keep your work and your family in balance by seeing both as special and sacred callings of God.

The Bible is clear that husbands and wives are to love and respect each other. As parents they are supposed to encourage rather than frustrate their children, who have a responsibility before God to obey their parents (it's all in Ephesians 5 and 6). From what the Bible says, these responsibilities continue as long as you are—a) married; b) still have kids around; c) still have parents around; or d) any of the above—which is basically your entire life.

Now, you probably knew that. It figures that God wants us to pay attention to the details of our family relationships. But did you know that God also cares about your work? Absolutely. God isn't some old-fashioned, out of touch, gray-haired Being who doesn't know what you're all about and what you're going through. He knows everything about you and your relationships, and you can be sure He knows about your work.

He knows that you probably spend half your waking hours in a job, and He knows how important that job is to your livelihood and your self-esteem. Your work matters to God.

That's why the Bible tells us, "Settle down and get to

work. Earn your own living. And I say to the rest of you. . .never get tired of doing good" (2 Thessalonians 3:12-13). Whether you're flipping burgers or writing computer code, you have the opportunity every day to show your boss, your coworkers, and your subordinates just how much God matters to you. And the best way to do that is to work to the best of your ability with the highest integrity every single day.

. . .In the Small Stuff

- Your work family is important, but it should never become more important than your real family.

- Your coworkers should know you're a Christian by your actions more than your words.

- There will be times when the demands of work will overshadow your family. Make sure your family knows this is only temporary.

- After a busy season at work, schedule a weekend away or a mini-vacation with your family.

As he was packing his meager possessions
to move out on his own,
the son looked fondly (and enviously)
around his parents' home.
As he gazed at the house, the furniture,
the yard, and the food, he asked,
"Dad, why would I leave all of this?"
His dad quickly replied,
"Because it is not yours!"

THIRTY-TWO
LETTING GO

If you have already had a child leave home, you know what we are about to discuss. If it hasn't happened to you yet, get ready. It won't be easy.

God helps prepare parents for this transition by making the kids go through the teenage years. Those can be trying years for a parent. There may be times when you doubt if your teenagers will ever leave home. . .because you might strangle them first. But as the actual time approaches, whether it is "off to college" or just "moving out on your own," both parent and child get an overwhelming sense that this event marks a transition in their relationship. The change of circumstances brings about an immediate change in the dynamic of the parent/child relationship. From this point forward, your relationship will be drastically different, and there will be no going back.

There will be mixed emotions as you "let go." You will struggle between *what you want* versus *what is best for your child.*

All of a sudden you will want your child to stay. Your child's irritating habits will suddenly become endearing traits. You will want the dirty laundry piled in the bedroom. You will want the bathroom to be a mess. You will want the refrigerator door left open and the phone line occupied. (Well, maybe . . .)

But you will know that your child needs to leave. Keeping your child at home is what you want *for yourself,* but allowing your child to leave home is what you want *for your child.* And you will know that what you want for your child is more important than what you want for yourself.

You will not be alone with your feelings. God knows exactly how you will feel. He had a Child leave home, too. But

God knew in advance everything that would happen to His Child, and you will know nothing about what will occur in the life of your child. So, talk to God about it. You can pray about your child's past and about your child's future.

For the past, pray that God will give your child a selective memory. You want your child to remember your strengths and forget those times when you disappointed your child (and God). You want your child's recollections to be of "Kodak moments," or at least of memories when you were trying *your* best for *your child's* best.

For the future, pray that God will guide both of you in learning, understanding, and enjoying the evolution of your relationship. Pray that you can move gracefully from rule maker/enforcer to advice-giver. Pray that your mouth will move only after your ear has listened. Pray that God will change your language from *instructions* to *advice.* As for your child, pray that God will instill a realization that you have no greater interest than his or her well-being. Pray that your child will be inclined to ask for advice when necessary. Pray that your child will have the wisdom to know which advice is priceless and which advice is worthless.

No matter how much you have prepared for the day of "letting go," it won't be enough. You will have done a better job at preparing your child than preparing yourself. So don't forget to pray for yourself. Pray that you will have full confidence in God's promise that He can keep your life in *peace* even when it seems to be broken in *pieces*.

Before He formed the universe, God knew the day when your child would be leaving home. He has great plans to work in the life of your child—plans that require you to "let go." You need do your part, so God can finish His part.

...IN THE SMALL STUFF

- "Letting go" means shifting from *instruction* to *influence*.

- Moving out is an essential part of growing up.

- "Letting go" can be a matter of perspective:

  —You aren't kicking them out; you have raised them up.

  —You are no longer swatting on the bottom; you're patting on the back.

  —You aren't losing a child; you're gaining a bathroom.

W hat is causing the quarrels
and fights among you?
Isn't it the whole army of evil desires
at war within you?

James 4:1

FAMILY CHALLENGES

THIRTY-THREE
CONFLICT

Conflict between family members is common. But you already knew that. We conflict with our own family more than anyone else. Why is that?

Well, over your lifetime, you spend more time with your husband or your wife, your son or daughter, and your parents than any other group of people (at least you should). And you usually spend that time with them in relatively close spaces, like your house and car. In addition, a family usually has limited physical resources, so that most of us from an early age have had to share bathrooms and toys and brownies and TV channels with others in our family. Generally this works out just fine, but occasionally big fights erupt—usually over small stuff.

Just because you grow up and start a family of your own doesn't mean the conflicts stop. Sometimes they increase because you're on the other end of the family spectrum. Now you're the parent managing the conflict between your kids; now you're the husband or wife doing your best to resolve conflict with your spouse.

God knows about your conflicts, and He cares about them. More importantly, He cares about your relationships with others and your capacity to love them unconditionally (just like He loves you).

The primary source of conflict, according to God's Word, comes from within us. That's where the envy and selfishness originate. If we realize that, we can better deal with our own "evil desires"—even the small ones—by asking God to forgive us and help us truly love those who are closest to us.

Loving one another may seem like a simple solution, but it's the best one. Truly loving your brother or sister or spouse or parent means you set aside your own selfish desires and seek what's best for the other person. It means finding common goals as you discover what you have in common.

Conflict is never easy to deal with, but when it's

resolved, the bond between family members is stronger than ever. Try it and see for yourself.

...In the Small Stuff

* Conflict is a fact of family life, but so is conflict resolution.

* We are not born with the natural ability to resolve conflict. It takes study and practice.

* Like a referee in a game, learn to know the players and the rules before mediating family disputes.

* It's impossible to grow closer as a family unless you experience conflict.

God is our refuge and strength,
always ready to help in times of trouble.

Psalm 46:1

THIRTY-FOUR

CRISIS

No one wants to go through a crisis, but you can't insulate yourself from them. They often happen unexpectedly...and tragically. It might be severe financial reverses, or sickness, or even death. It may be rebellious children or a fractured marriage.

You may have no control over the events that trigger the crises in your family, but you have the choice of how you are going to respond. The manner in which you react to the crises could make matters better or worse. In the midst of calamity, you might not be thinking objectively. So now, in this quiet moment, let's consider how God could use a crisis for good in your family.

Tragedy could potentially splinter a family, but it

could also be the basis for bringing family members together. Adversity can be endured more easily with friends and family by your side. Lasting bonds of love and friendship can be forged through tough times because you "were there" for each other. Many people often shy away from family and friends in the midst of catastrophe because they don't know what to say. But the words aren't important. Your presence is all that may be required; your availability will speak from your heart the words that your mouth cannot say.

Just as difficult times can unite you with your family, a crisis may be the event that reconnects you with God. He often gets forgotten in the "good times" when you are thinking that you are self-sufficient. (While you might never say so, your actions might indicate that you think you have no need of God.) But when the money runs out, or your health is in jeopardy, or the children are in trouble, you can turn to God and He will be there. No appointment necessary. You don't have to take a number. And you won't get stuck with His voice mail. You can speak directly to Him, and He can make Himself known to you.

The tough times you endure can also be a way to prepare and equip your children to handle difficulties in their future. You wouldn't want your children to succumb to their problems with whining and self-pity, so don't let them catch you responding to your troubles that way. Your perseverance in the face of adversity is a lesson your children need to learn, and you can be the best teacher.

The devastation of any crisis will be minimized if you use it as an opportunity to bring your family closer to each other and to God.

...IN THE SMALL STUFF

- Answers to problems come easily if they are other people's problems.

- Some problems can be attacked, but others must be endured. All problems should be given to God.

- If we prayed more often to *keep out* of trouble, we wouldn't have to pray so much to *get out* of trouble.

- When the crisis is at its worst, then your life can only get better.

- The best way to reduce the size of your troubles is to compare them to the size of your blessings.

Divorce is an easy escape, many think.
But, in counseling many divorcees,
the guilt and loneliness they experience
can be even more tragic than
living with their problem.

THIRTY-FIVE
DIVORCE

We are living in an age of disposability. Everything from diapers to cameras to contact lenses can be used and then discarded. We use them once—or when we are tired of them, we toss them. With this type of mentality, we don't often place sentimental (or even practical) significance on many of the things in our lives. Sadly, this perspective has invaded our society's view of marriage, with the predictable result of divorce.

God intends marriage to be permanent. Jesus Himself said that since a husband and wife "are no longer two but one, let no one separate them, for God has joined them together" (Matthew 19:6). This means that young couples might have to change their perspective about marriage before they enter it. They should not view marriage as a hobby that can be tried and abandoned when their interest in it (or in each other) wanes.

And for those already in marriage, they need to work as hard at keeping the marriage together as they worked to get married in the first place. For them divorce should not even be an option, and they need to sense God's desire that they make every effort toward continual and mutual forgiveness and restoration.

But for many people, divorce has already occurred in their lives. Are they doomed to experience less than a good life because of their failed marriage? Just because they have chosen (or had forced upon them) a circumstance which is not God's preference, they are not stuck living in an inferior "Plan B" world. God does not reserve His love only for those who follow His intended "Plan A." And aren't we glad of that, because every one of us has stepped outside of Plan A. We may not all have been divorced, but we have all disappointed and failed God. And while God hates divorce, He also hates our lying, and our pride, and any disrespect or unkindness we show to our spouse even if we remain married.

We have a God who is in the business of restoring relationships. The most *important* relationship is ours with Him. While we can reject Him quickly and frequently, He is always ready to forgive and receive us back into fellowship with Him. He never abandons us. He never quits on us. He never gives up on us.

God's unconditional love is the model He wants us to use for marriage. So, in our age of disposability, let's not look at marriages as something that can be discarded or recycled.

…IN THE SMALL STUFF

- Keep looking for ways to restore your marriage instead of looking for reasons to leave it.

- If a marriage was founded only on love at first sight, it is likely to end by divorce at first thought.

- Some people give more thought to choosing a divorce attorney than to restoring their marriage.

- Divorce can happen if people want their own way instead of God's way.

- Yes, God hates divorce. But He also hates a proud and hypocritical attitude in those who refuse to recognize that their own sins are equally displeasing to Him.

To be able to blend is to have
blendable components from the start.

Jim Smoke

THIRTY-SIX

BLENDED FAMILIES

Conventional wisdom tells you that the biggest challenges for human beings involve things like getting perfect scores on your college entrance exams, climbing the world's highest mountains, turning bankrupt companies around, or competing in the Olympics. Don't be fooled. Those activities pale when compared to life's greatest challenge: blending two families together.

According to Jim Smoke, in his book, *Growing in Remarriage*, blending families is essentially bringing the lifestyles of two different people and their families together. As you can imagine—or as you know, if you've been there—it's a process in which the two family life-styles will either "collide or merge."

That's because individual and family life-styles involve "hundreds—perhaps thousands—of little things that combine to describe how any of us live our lives in today's world." One person is neat while the other is messy. Some people are just naturally punctual, while others are always late. There are motivated people in this world, and then there are those who are, well, more relaxed. It's hard enough learning to get along when those various personality types crop up in one family, let alone when two families with different life-styles come together in a new blended family.

Whether you are about to enter the world of the blended family, or you've been there for a while now, Dr. Smoke advises family members to—

- be patient—you won't blend overnight;
- be aware—enter into the experience with your eyes open;
- be tolerant—you all have different personalities, and one isn't better than the other.

It's also important to realize that there will be a certain amount of "yours, mine, and ours" in a blended family.

Avoid showing favoritism and try instead to achieve balance, whether you're disciplining or rewarding a family member. Most important, realize that God knows every single detail of everyone's life. And even though He's not big on divorce, He will bless those who make Him the center of their blended families.

...IN THE SMALL STUFF

* Before you blend two families, talk to others who have done it successfully.

* The chances of families blending successfully increase greatly if God is already at the center of both families.

* Blending doesn't mean you lose the individual personalities that make your families unique.

* It's important to blend two families into one church so you can worship together.

Long illnesses are good schools of mercy
for those who tend the sick,
and of loving patience
for those who suffer.

Jean Pierre Camus

If you've ever faced a severe illness with someone in your family, then you know what it's like to experience the ultimate agony. Nothing compares with the pain and anguish you feel when someone very dear to you is suffering a physical malady, especially if it seems there is no cure or hope.

We don't see the big picture, of course. We assume that because someone seems helpless, then they are also hopeless. We tend to equate pain with evil, and freedom from pain with ultimate bliss.

Actually, there is truth in that assumption. The Bible is very clear that evil—including physical pain and death—is the result of humanity's sinful rebellion against God. But it's not as if God is punishing us for our sins. Rather, we are experiencing the effects of our rebellion, which will continue until God makes things right again.

So why don't we all get sick and suffer in this life? Why do some children go through painful illnesses, while some bad people seem to do just fine? King David even reflected on this when he wrote, "For I envied the proud when I saw them prosper despite their wickedness. They seem to live such a painless life; their bodies are so healthy and strong" (Psalm 73:3-4).

We don't have an answer for that, except to tell you that God will help you in a time of family illness, regardless of how mild or severe it is. He cares about your physical condition, and He guarantees that if your spiritual condition is good, then you will be able to better handle physical adversity.

Please understand us. There are no guarantees that the illness will go away, although God is still the God who heals. All we are saying is that you will be able to deal with any illness in your family without losing faith—even if you don't understand it—if you truly believe that God always wants the best for you.

What you can absolutely count on is that someday

when you and your family members are with God in heaven, the physical pain and even death itself will cease. By accepting the sacrifice of Jesus, God's only Son, on your behalf and for your sin, you will have eternal life with "no more death or sorrow or crying or pain" (Revelation 21:4).

...IN THE SMALL STUFF

- It's dangerous to think that God causes illness to punish us.

- It's healthy to believe that God uses illness to teach us.

- Show compassion to family members who are sick, and they'll do the same for you.

- Thank God first when the illness passes; then thank your doctor.

- Prayer changes things, especially when it comes to illness.

I hate death. In fact,
I could live forever without it.

Pogo

THIRTY-EIGHT

DEATH

You can tell that our society is uncomfortable with death by all of the euphemisms for it: passed away; expired; gone; the grand finale; curtains; six feet under. People actually *fear* death because they don't know what it means or what, if anything, happens next. But their fear is unnecessary because the Bible explains everything they need to know.

God has placed within each of us an eternal soul. From the moment of our conception, that soul exists forever. Our physical death is merely the cessation of our biological being, but our soul lives on. This should be a great encouragement to all us because it means that death is not the end. *However* (didn't you just know this was coming?) our destination for eternity cannot be changed after we die.

We like to say that eternity has two sections: smoking and non-smoking. You have probably heard them referred to as "Hell" and "Heaven." Another way of looking at it would be: spending eternity separated from God (Hell), or spending eternity with Him (Heaven).

The Bible tells us that Heaven will be a wonderful place, with no sadness or sickness. It will be better than we can even imagine because we will be in the presence of God. Hell will be the opposite. Separation from God will mean suffering and torment.

Don't be fooled by those who think there is no Hell because a loving God couldn't send people there. God doesn't send people to Hell, but they can end up there because they chose to reject Him during their lifetime. If, during your lifetime, you establish a personal relationship with God through His Son, Jesus, then you are set for Heaven in your life after death. On the other hand, if you reject Jesus during your life, then you are choosing to spend your eternity after death separated from God. It is your choice.

This is the real significance of death: Not that it is the finale to life, but that it is the end of your opportunity to make a choice for God.

...In the Small Stuff

- Death is not the end of your life's story; it is just the end of a chapter.

- When we die, we leave everything behind except the choice we made about God during our life.

- You should fear dying until you make arrangements with God for life after death.

- Going to God in death is better than staying here without Him.

- There is no second chance after death. . .just the consequences of your first chance.

Show me thy ways,
O LORD; teach me thy paths.

Psalm 25:4 (KJV)

FAMILY IMPROVEMENT

THIRTY-NINE
EDUCATION

The importance of education cannot be overemphasized. But people often confuse schooling with education. There are some similarities, but there are some significant differences.

Schooling usually ends after twelve to sixteen years. You start at kindergarten and you stop when you get your diploma. But an education should be a continual, lifelong process. You begin learning as a child, and hopefully the process doesn't ever stop. If you have an attitude of learning throughout your life, then you stay inquisitive. Boredom won't be a worry for you if you are always looking to acquire knowledge about new subjects.

Schooling usually has a set of curricula; there are

established subjects and majors. You may have some electives, but your choices are limited to what is offered by the school. Your education, however, has no such limitations. Your education is limited only by your own curiosity.

Schooling happens in the classroom, but your education is not limited to what you learn within the four walls of an educational institution.

Schooling often focuses on learning from textbooks, but an education can be gained from life itself. In the classroom, you might learn historical facts or mathematical formulas. Your education includes what you can learn from people, places, and circumstances.

Schooling is not a family activity, but education can be. Many lessons about life can be learned during family activities. In this context, opportunities will arise to learn (and teach) lessons about relationships, attitudes, and perspectives.

When you consider that God has the events in your life under His watchful eye, you realize that He can bring into your life the things that you need to learn. Of course, you need to be living life with the expectation of learning from it. Look at life as an opportunity to obtain the education that God has in store for you. After all, what you learn in life is tuition-free.

…IN THE SMALL STUFF

- Be a student of life.

- In every new and difficult situation, ask yourself: "What can I learn from this?"

- The more you learn about God, the more you will learn about yourself.

- Most of life's most important lessons can only be learned outside of the classroom.

O! had I but followed the arts!

Sir Andrew, in *Twelfth Night*
by William Shakespeare

.

FORTY
THE ARTS

There is a place where entertainment and education come together. It's called the arts. At least that's our loose definition. Normally you hear people describe the arts as a branch of learning, such as history, literature, philosophy, music, and medicine. But that seems way too stuffy and formal, like you have to be enrolled in a university or have a doctor's degree to appreciate them.

We think the arts are for the whole family, and they don't have to be stuffy. If you approach them right and find the fascinating and relevant aspects of music, literature, painting, science, and history, you will encourage your family to participate in a lifetime of learning. As a result, you and your family will come to appreciate those things in this life that really count.

Together you will discover that music didn't originate with Elvis or hip-hop. Rather, Christian music came out of the Psalms, which were the praises of God's people for His goodness. You'll find that the great themes of literature point to the need to find meaning in life through God. The history of painting will sparkle as you observe the glorious themes of the Bible portrayed by master artists. Science will come alive as it demonstrates the intelligent design, the beauty, and the order of God's created universe.

Yes, there are themes of darkness and despair throughout human history and in the arts, especially in the last century. Don't shield your family from these instructive images and events. Instead, teach your children to recognize the misery and hopelessness of a world in rebellion to God.

You can discover the arts in museums and concert halls, of course, and we encourage you to expose your family to these "finer" things as often as you can. But you don't have to go to the big city to enjoy the arts. Build a library of classic literature and classical music in your home. Collect art, history, and science books. There are some wonderful and inexpensive resources available.

Already we're impressed with your commitment to bring these good things into your home. You're reading this book, aren't you? While we don't pretend to be accomplished authors or artists, the least we can do is encourage you to discover the great ones for yourself.

...In the Small Stuff

* Don't think for a minute that you're in the minority when it comes to enjoying the arts. More people attend cultural events each year than sporting events.

* While it's true that the media contains culture, you have to look awfully hard to find it.

* The more effort you put out, the more you will appreciate the arts.

* It's a fact: Classical music helps you think better (and it helps your plants grow, too).

An investment in knowledge
pays the best interest.

Benjamin Franklin

FORTY-ONE
COLLEGE

Why is it that most families have mixed feelings about college? Most of us attended college; some are *still* attending college. Yet when it comes to thinking about our kids going to college, our hearts race with white-knuckle intensity.

Part of the anxiety comes from concerns over the cost. For years financial planners have frightened families with horror stories about the price of higher education, how it's going to cost a year's salary to send your kid to college—for one year! So you better put away a thousand dollars a month for the rest of your life just to pay for the books.

In our experience, it's not all that bad. Look at it this way: When we went to college, a year of tuition, room, and board at a typical private college cost about as much as a new car. Today, a year of college runs about as much. . .as a new car. So you drive your used car a little longer, make a few sacrifices for a while, and you put your kids through college. No big deal.

The other concern about college comes from the colleges themselves. Like our public secondary schools, they've written God out of the curriculum. And the public colleges and universities have gone one step further. They have created an environment that is hostile to Christianity. In fact, the Christian world view is the only world view that is unacceptable on most college campuses today.

Fortunately, there are many excellent private colleges and universities that continue to uphold biblical values. They don't water down the learning. They simply present all truth through the perspective of a Christian world view, which at its most basic level acknowledges that God exists.

We're not saying that every Christian kid should go to a Christian college. We need Christian students in our secular colleges and universities. (It's that salt and light principle.) But there are educational alternatives available for families who want their kids to learn in an environment where God is included.

Whatever you do, invest a lot of time in prayer. Invite

God into the details of the college selection process. You'll be amazed at the results.

…In the Small Stuff

- When it comes time for someone in your family to choose a college, encourage him or her to personally visit as many campuses as possible.

- Get involved in the college selection process, but don't interfere.

- If you've ever thought about going back to college, don't think any more. *Do it!*

- There's nothing wrong with questioning the so-called Judeo-Christian value system, but you should never let someone get by with throwing it out.

- There's no rule that says you have to stop learning when you finish college.

Wherever your treasure is,
there your heart and thought will also be.

Matthew 6:211

FORTY-TWO

MONEY MANAGEMENT

You can talk about what is important to you, but your true priorities will be revealed by how you handle your finances. And those around you may not pay attention to what you are saying, but they will certainly notice how you spend your money. This can be a real case of cash receipts talking louder than words.

Your personal finances are, in fact, a convenient way to judge the kind of person you are. A brief examination of your spending habits may disclose more about you than you wish to know:

- You might consider yourself to be generous, but that is

not really the case if you can walk by the Salvation Army Christmas donation bucket without flinching.

- Maybe you think that you are free from materialism, but that probably isn't the case if you have the Home Shopping Channel toll-free number on your phone's speed dial.

- And you aren't very charitable if you turn off the lights in the house and don't answer the doorbell when the Girl Scouts come to sell cookies.

Not only do your finances provide you with a mirror to your heart, they also provide you with an excellent teaching tool. As with many aspects of life, your conduct can be a good example or a poor one. Fortunately, we can choose what kind of example we wish to be. So, for example, if we want to reflect that God has priority in our life, then we will want to acknowledge that priority by returning some of our wealth to Him. Now, He doesn't need it, and we can't make a check directly payable to "God" (or if we do, we aren't really sincere because we know it won't get cashed), but there are ministries which can use our money to help the poor.

Self-reflection and self-examination from time to time are good things. But don't just contemplate yourself in your mind. Actually pull out that checkbook and see where you have been spending your money. It will be time well spent to determine if your money was well spent.

...IN THE SMALL STUFF

* You can tell a lot about the priorities in your life by looking at your checkbook.

* True charity doesn't care if it is tax deductible.

* It is better to spend your money on *experiences* for your family than on *things* for them.

* Don't give to God because He needs it. Give to God because He deserves it.

* Whether you have a lot or a little, the quality of your life is not determined by the quantity in your life.

Show respect for everyone.
Love your Christian brothers and sisters.
Fear God.

1 Peter 2:17

FAMILY RESPONSIBILITY

FORTY-THREE
RESPECT

You hear a lot about respect these days, often in the context of competition. Before the Big Game, an athlete will say, "Last time we played the Hornets, they didn't give us the respect we deserved." Such a statement implies that you should respect someone because of his or her ability. But that goes more to the nature of admiration. You *admire* someone because they can do something you never could, but you don't necessarily respect them.

Respect has more to do with honor and appreciation. The first time you heard the word was probably when someone told you to "respect your elders." This advice is common to all cultures (some more than others), because it really is a good idea to honor and appreciate those who are older and wiser than we are.

Another aspect of respect has to do with having a high regard for someone because they are in authority over us. Unfortunately, this kind of respect has been watered down for various reasons, most having to do with the breakdown of authority in many places. People don't respect the law or law enforcement officials like they used to. Respect for teachers, bosses, and the clergy has dropped. And parenthood is the Rodney Dangerfield of professions: Parents get no respect.

Just in case you are feeling bad over losing the respect of your students, employees, parishioners, or children, consider this: Respect for God has diminished over the years as well, to the point where people today are quite skeptical of an all-powerful, all-knowing, all-loving God who is intimately involved in the universe and our lives.

Some social observers may applaud this loss of respect in our world, thinking it puts us all on a level playing field. We happen to disagree. If you remove from our society respect for age, experience, authority (both civil and moral), and learning, then the only sort of respect you have left is for ability. And when you do that, you reduce respect to competition, which means that the only ones worthy of respect are those who can shoot more baskets or earn more money than everyone else.

You know very well that in your family it just doesn't work that way. That's not how you earn respect. To the contrary, you earn respect as a parent by having high regard for your children. As you care for them, keep them safe, teach them, and love them unconditionally, you will gain the respect of your kids. There's no yelling, no demanding (except on rare occasions with teenagers), and not even any competition (well, don't kid yourself—parents compete all the time for respect).

If you want your parents to respect you (no matter how old you are), first give them honor and esteem and obedience. Don't wait for them to perform the way you want them to, and by all means, don't reduce them to asking for your respect. Give it to them from your heart, even if it's uncomfortable.

Finally, here's a suggestion on how to gain the respect of everyone around you. Show ultimate respect for God. Who else in your life is worthy of more honor and praise than the One who created you, the One who loves you, and the One who knows you better than anyone? As you show respect for God in how you talk about Him, how you express your love for Him, how you read His Word, and how you pray to Him, you will encourage others in your family to do the same.

...IN THE SMALL STUFF

* It's good to respect God for what He does. It's even better to respect God for who He is.

* Like all moral values, respect is *caught* more than it is *taught*.

* That said, make it a point to model respect more often than you teach it.

* By teaching your kids to properly respect authority when they're young, they will feel more secure as they grow up.

* Children who respect their elders are easier to live with.

* You earn respect for yourself by showing respect to others.

Few things help an individual more
than to place responsibility upon him,
and to let him know that you trust him.

Booker T. Washington

RESPONSIBILITIES

Living in a family brings responsibilities to everyone. Many families only think of the parents as having responsibilities, but that is a huge mistake. If children don't learn to accept and assume responsibility at a young age, they will be more apt to avoid it when they are older.

Why are parents often remiss when it comes to teaching responsibility to their children? We can think of two possible reasons:

1. *Some parents think that the imposition of responsibilities will alienate their children.* Parents are concerned about protecting their children from negative influences. They worry about what their children are doing, and whom they are doing it with.

These parents recognize that their children often come close to crossing the line of acceptable behavior and friends. Out of fear that their children might rebel against assigned chores and duties, these parents abstain from assigning responsibilities to their children. What a tragedy, and what a contradiction! In an attempt to protect their children, these parents are not preparing their children for the future. These children are left vulnerable and ill-prepared to accept and shoulder the responsibilities they will find in their future jobs and families.

2. *Some parents may be too busy to impose responsibilities upon their children.* Time is required to give your children chores and assignments: adequate explanation and instruction takes time; monitoring their performance takes time; evaluating the quality of their work takes time; and time is required for rewards (or discipline) as appropriate. But in many families, parental time is in short supply. It may be easier, and certainly quicker, to "do it yourself" or "not do it at all" than to assign it to the children. But this attitude places a higher value on the *parent's time* than on the *child's character.* Time will always be limited, but the opportunity for building the character of your child is fleeting.

Responsibility is a character trait that will produce

strong families (and a strong society). But responsibility doesn't happen by accident. It isn't acquired from a parent's wishful thinking or good intentions. Responsibility comes as the result of years of character training. It is developed gradually. If it is not nurtured in your home, you will be stunting your child's growth.

...IN THE SMALL STUFF

* Only a few people take responsibility; the rest of them just want to take the credit.

* Accountability to God produces responsibility in life.

* We may not be responsible for what happens to us, but we are responsible for how we respond to it.

* It is parents' responsibility to teach their children responsibility.

* Your children's success or failure in life will be determined in large part by how they handle their responsibilities.

An honest answer
is like a kiss on the lips.

Proverbs 24:26 (NIV)

HONESTY

Honesty in a family is an amazing thing. When family members are truthful with each other in love, special bonds develop that can never be broken. Honesty is like some kind of super glue that keeps a husband and wife, parents and children, and brothers and sisters closely knit and very much in love.

On the other hand, dishonesty and deceit can tear the fabric of a family apart. A false phrase may be sweet to the taste at first, but eventually the untruthful words will churn like spoiled food in your stomach until you feel like throwing up.

There are no excuses for dishonesty, but there are plenty of motives. We have some things to hide and we don't want anyone—especially anyone in our family—to find out. Or we want something from another person, so we butter them up with phony compliments. And sometimes we think we need to "protect" someone else by telling him or her a little lie. None of these motives lead to any good. Worse, they lead to embarrassment, anger, and a loss of trust, which is awfully hard to get back.

Honesty is at the root of so much that's good about our lives: love, respect, contentment, joy (go ahead, add to the list). So why do we think dishonesty is ever a good idea? That's hard to say, but we all lie and eventually suffer the unfortunate consequences, which usually include hurting those who are closest to us.

There are so many benefits to honesty we should be amazed and ashamed that we don't make it our ongoing policy. Here are just a few. (Again, feel free to add to our list.)

- Honesty leads to trust.

- When you're honest, you feel lighter because you aren't carrying around that extra weight of guilt.

- Honest people are healthier people.

- Being honest saves you time because you don't have to spend extra hours covering your tracks.

- Honest people sleep better.

- When you're faced with a decision between telling the truth or telling a lie, carefully weigh the benefits of honesty with the consequences of deceit.

Be strong and of a good courage.

Deuteronomy 31:23 (KJV)

FORTY-FIVE

ENCOURAGEMENT

Most people think that encouragement is nothing more than positive words spoken to uplift, comfort, and inspire. Well, that's partly correct. But sincere and effective encouragement must be more than a vocabulary list of motivational terminology gleaned from one of those infomercial salesman with an overactive thyroid gland.

If you want your encouragement to be effective, it must be honest. Don't try to motivate your child with false praise about being the best player on the team if there is a permanent indentation on the bench where your child sat all season long. Your children will not be encouraged by comments that they know are dishonest. In fact, it will make them feel even worse. They will assume that they are so worthless that you are forced to lie to think of something good to say about them.

You should always be ready with a word of encouragement when it is needed, but you shouldn't be cavalier about it. Effective encouragement might require quite a bit of creativity on your part. You have to know exactly what to say. . .and how to say it. . .and when to say it. In times of discouragement, your family members may be particularly sensitive and defensive. Timing and phrasing are important. An encouraging word, spoken at the wrong time or with the wrong inflection, might be misinterpreted as sarcasm or criticism.

Effective encouragement also requires a proper environment. Encouragement doesn't come naturally in homes where there is hostility and cynicism. In an antagonistic environment, people are too wrapped up in tearing each other down to bother with building each other up. In contrast, a loving home *fosters* encouragement. In that type of environment, your family will feel secure and appreciated. When a loving attitude pervades the home, each family member is encouraged without words even being spoken because they have a sense of self-worth. . .they know they are loved by their family and by God because of *who* they are and not because of *what* they have accomplished. They are free to tackle new challenges, and free to fail in the attempt, because they are fully confident that they will have the support of their family.

As you think about encouraging your family, don't rely just on words. Look for other ways to communicate what you want to say. Remember, sometimes your heart needs to speak louder than your mouth.

...In the Small Stuff

* Encouragement is anatomical:

    —It sometimes requires a pat on the back;

    —It sometimes means a kick in the rear;

    —It always seems to lift the chin and straighten the shoulders.

* Correction is instructional; encouragement is motivational.

* Encouragement costs nothing, and yet it pays tremendous dividends.

If you refuse to discipline your children,
it proves you don't love them;
if you love your children,
you will be prompt to discipline them.

Proverbs 13:24

FORTY-SIX

DISCIPLINE

Many families are so contemporary that they no longer practice what has become the lost art of our ancestors. No, we aren't talking about quilting. Somewhere in the past few decades we have lost the art of child discipline. Oh, it's not that we have abandoned the concept of discipline altogether. But we apply it selectively. We love discipline as a "positive mental attitude" (such as "I'll discipline myself to jog three miles each day"). But we have pretty much abandoned any politically incorrect concept of correcting a child's misbehavior with discipline (such as "I won't tell my son he can't dismantle the television set because I wouldn't want to squelch his innate curiosity").

Although the concept may seem old fashioned, the Bible says that parents who love their children will discipline them. It is a vital part of parental responsibility. Without correction, children will grow up with no clear understanding of behavioral boundaries. A lack of discipline suggests that the parents have little regard for the child's character development.

Many parents are reluctant to discipline because they don't want to stifle their child's creativity. This philosophy, however, shows a misunderstanding of behavior and discipline. Discipline is for the purpose of developing the child's sense of good and evil, right and wrong. Some behavior, although creative, is just plain wrong and needs to be stifled. But discipline does not require inactivity. In fact, discipline should not convey that "good" means immobility and "evil" means activity. It is not the goal of discipline to produce sedate and passive children. Discipline should channel creativity and enthusiasm into productive and beneficial activities.

No one ever said that child discipline was easy (and now, it is not even socially acceptable). It takes time and patience to design a plan of discipline that will teach and correct your children without exasperating them or causing them to be angry or discouraged. And just when you find a technique that works, then they outgrow it, and you have to go back to the discipline drawing board.

Take heart! Your consistent, loving discipline will ultimately teach your children to discipline themselves. Then your job will be easier.

...In the Small Stuff

- Early discipline averts future disaster.

- It is better for a parent to impose limits when children are young than for a judge to impose a sentence when they are older.

- Sometimes "learning at your mother's knee" requires being bent over it.

- Don't discipline if you are frustrated or angry. Your only attitude in discipline should be love.

- The lasting impression of discipline will be God's character in your child's life, not your hand on her bottom.

I was hard to have a conversation with anyone,
there were too many people talking.

Yogi Berra

FORTY-SEVEN

COMMUNICATION

No two families talk to each other in the same way. Some families communicate through audible signals. For example, some years ago, we discovered that each of our families had developed a distinct whistling sound, which we use whenever we can't find each other in a public place, like a large store. It isn't one of those shrill, put-all-your-fingers-in-your-mouth-and-blow kind of whistles, but a bird-like call that our families immediately recognize.

You may not like our little communication signals. You may be like some families, who greet each other with enthusiastic shouts and big bear hugs. Or your family may be among those who stretch out their arms quietly, preferring to pat each other on the back and whisper loving words.

Of course, not all family communication is warm and enthusiastic. Sometimes families go through cold and quiet periods, where icy comments replace light-hearted banter. But those times are usually few and far between, because if there's one thing families have to do, it's communicate.

The trick is to communicate in healthy, productive ways, which isn't as easy as it sounds. Like anything worthwhile, positive communication takes practice and effort. It may be that someone in the family needs to "facilitate" by modeling good communication skills (and that someone may be you).

We certainly aren't communication experts, but we've seen what works in our families. Here are some ideas you may want to try:

- *Meal Conversation.* Sitting down as a family for a meal is a rarity these days, so take advantage of the time (you probably need to schedule these times by putting them on the calendar each week). Turn off the television, put on some nice music, light a candle, and begin with prayer. Invite God to be in your conversation.

Then invite everyone at the table to talk about whatever is on their mind.

- *Family Meetings.* These won't happen all that often, but family meetings are useful when a big decision needs to be made or a crisis is brewing. Or you may just want to plan a special time so you can catch up on what everyone is doing and planning. Someone needs to "moderate." (Don't worry, you don't need to use *Roberts Rule of Order*, although you should try to be orderly.)

- *Family Vacations.* Planning and taking regular family vacations isn't as easy as it used to be. When we were young, a weekend camping trip was easy to throw together at the last minute. Today you need a reservation months in advance, even if you're going to Fred's Campground and Bait Shop. And everyone in the family has a full calendar of activities that need to be cleared. But don't let that dissuade you! Your family needs those weekends away and occasional two-week vacations so you can experience the complete spectrum of family communication—from pure joy to utter confusion to total chaos.

There's one more aspect of family communication that families rarely practice: *listening.* Maybe it's because from the time we are babies we all learn that the only way to get anything is to *yell.* Well, that may work for helpless infants, but the rest of us need to work on our listening skills. Besides giving you valuable information you usually miss by talking louder than everyone else, listening also communicates to others in the family that you really care about them.

Make no mistake about it. Listening, like all forms of effective communication, takes effort. Listening is work. But the results can be incredible as you help others with their needs while fulfilling your own.

…IN THE SMALL STUFF

* Learn to recognize the non-verbal signals of your family members.

- Playing games together as a family encourages communication (as long as they're not video games).

- Watching television as a family does *not* constitute communication.

- Do these three things if you want to become a good communicator: *listen, laugh, love.*

They were amazed at his teaching,
for [Jesus] taught as one
who had real authority.

Mark 1:22

FORTY-EIGHT

AUTHORITY

Your household can't run efficiently without someone in charge. There needs to be a chain of command. Someone has got to be in charge. However, the question of "Who's the Boss?" can be a point of contention that disrupts the harmony in your home.

Our humble suggestion is that you let God be the authority in your home. We know that sounds trite and is easy to say, but it is exactly the arrangement God designed. Notice the ramifications of this approach.

On issues of disagreement between a husband and wife, neither one gets to have it "his way" or "her way." There won't be the drawing of battle lines. There won't be one winner and one loser. Instead, both the husband and wife can agree to see what God has to say about the issue. Of course, God won't always speak specifically to each issue. (For instance, He probably won't tell you whether you should buy a Toyota instead of a Honda.) But the Bible has clear guidelines in many practical areas, such as money management. And even if the answer to a specific question can't be found in the Bible, God can work in the hearts and minds of the husband and wife as they pray and read the Bible together. They submit to the authority of God in their family when they are willing to accept His decision (instead of their own) on the issue.

Placing God as the authority in the home has an advantage for parents. The parents don't have to become the final arbiters on many issues. Instead, the family can agree that they will look to God (through the Bible) to decide contested issues. The Bible speaks clearly on issues such as behavior, attitude, and influences. Parents and children often have a difference of opinion on these issues, and either one could be taking an extreme position. Instead of arguing, they should agree to see if God has anything to say on the issue and, if so, to let that be the final decision. In addition to finding the answer, both the parent and child will spiritually benefit from the practice of submitting to God's authority.

When God is the authority in the home, your family can be a partnership of equals. Oh, sure, the husband, wife, and children will have different roles, but they can trust each other, knowing that each person functions in the family under God's leadership and authority.

...IN THE SMALL STUFF

* Many people want authority without responsibility.

* There is always authority in the family. It is just a question of who exercises it.

* Some people handle authority well and grow in the process; others misuse authority and just over-inflate.

* It is better to learn submission to authority in the backyard than the prison yard.

* Authority in the home is like a bottle of fine wine. It increases in value if you don't have to use it.

Good manners is the art of making
those people easy with
whom we converse.

Jonathan Swift

Manners are a lost art. Unless you grew up in the South, or your mother happens to be Judith Martin (AKA Miss Manners, the syndicated newspaper columnist), it's likely that you've never cracked a book of etiquette.

Not that you're an unmannerly person. You're not lewd, rude, or disgusting, and you're doing your best to help your family follow your example. You mind your own business, you give other people lots of room (in checkout lines, on the highway, in relationships), and you're especially kind to animals and old people.

Terrific. You have good manners. Or do you? Aren't you simply taking a passive rather than active approach to manners? In other words, you equate being polite and courteous with *not* acting rudely. But what are you doing to proactively use good manners in all situations?

The difference is that when you display good manners, you do more than avoid doing what comes naturally—such as telling people off, making sarcastic remarks behind their backs, and going for days without shaving. You actually do things that add value to your relationships. Think of it this way. Whenever you interact with another person—especially someone in your family—try to see that person as God sees them: someone who has value because they have been created in God's image.

Jesus made a very strong statement for good manners when He said, "Love your neighbor as yourself" (Matthew 22:39). So who is your neighbor? Jesus said your neighbor is anyone in need (which covers just about everybody). And how do you love your neighbor as yourself? Simply put, you want the best for them.

You are courteous, you are kind and polite, and you have fun *with* other people rather than at their expense. Even more important—and this is what it means to have an *active* approach to manners—you offer to help if the other person is in need.

If you want to read a great illustration of this principle, review the story of the Good Samaritan (Luke 10:30-37). Jesus told this story as an example of what it means to be someone's neighbor, and we think it perfectly illustrates what it means to have good manners.

...IN THE SMALL STUFF

* Good manners show respect for others.

* Good manners demonstrate self-respect.

* Be as good-mannered to people behind their backs as you are in their presence.

* Just because manners are a lost art doesn't mean that you can't help your family develop an artistic flair for etiquette.

* If it doesn't bother you to offend others, at least refrain from offending yourself.

T rust in the Lord with all your heart;
do not depend on your own understanding.
Seek his will in all you do,
and he will direct your paths.

Proverbs 3:5–6

FORTY-NINE

DECISION MAKING

Y ou should protect your children from many things, but don't protect them so much that they miss the opportunity to make decisions. Decision making is a skill that must be developed. And part of the learning process includes making a few wrong decisions. Isn't it better to allow your children to make a few "wrong decisions" when the consequences are relatively minor and you are around to assist in the learning process? Don't let your children's first confrontation and struggle with major decisions come after they have left home.

The best way to teach your children about decision making is to model it for them. Let them watch you go through the process. Of course, this means you have to let them know a little bit about what's going on in the family (and that might not be too bad either). The decision might be as momentous as whether you should change careers, or it could be as mundane as whether to buy a new car. (Of course, you can have a little fun with this. Tell your teenagers you're thinking about buying a car, and they'll get all excited. Then tell them the car is a 1984 Dodge Diplomat, and watch their faces go pale.) The important point is to let them see how you approach the decision. . . whether you make a list of the "pros" and "cons," or whether you research information, or whether you ask the advice of others. (Of course, this presupposes that you actually have a process for making decisions. If you don't, then that's your mistake, and your children can learn the consequences of random selection.)

Including your child in the process is the best *method* to teach them decision making, but the most important *principle* to teach them about decision making is to include God in the process. Don't let them think that God is only interested in the major decisions of life. ("What job should I take?" "Whom should I marry?") Show them that God is interested in the smallest details of our lives. Just as you care *where* they go, *who* they're with, and *what* they're doing, so does God. And He is available to guide them in each of those daily decisions that they will be making.

At some point, your children will be on their own facing significant decisions. You probably won't be available (or asked) to give your opinion. But you can do something *now* that will help your children *then*. Let them make some of their own decisions now, so they can learn that God needs to be part of the process.

...IN THE SMALL STUFF

* Freedom is the ability to make decisions. Wisdom is the ability to make the *right* decisions.

* Your children won't learn how to make the right decisions unless you give them enough freedom to make the wrong ones.

* Your decisions are likely to end with problems if you don't consult with God at the start.

* Indecision is often a decision in itself.

* Decisions made too quickly can leave you stuck with consequences that last a lifetime.

In nature there are neither rewards nor punishments—there are consequences.

Robert G. Ingersoll

FIFTY
CONSEQUENCES

One of the fundamental truths of the natural world is that every action has a reaction. Another way to say this is that every cause has an effect. The same principle applies to human behavior. We're not psychologists (maybe that's a good thing), but our general observation has been that all choices have consequences. Think about that statement and see if you don't agree.

Let's start on a simple level and take an example of something you do routinely, and that's brush your teeth (at least we hope it's routine). You *choose* to brush your teeth—nobody's forcing you—because you want the *consequences* of a healthy mouth and good breath. (Okay, some of us need industrial strength mouthwash, too.) You could also choose not to brush your teeth, which would, of course, produce some undesirable consequences.

The same exercise could apply to all kinds of small choices you make every day, hundreds of times a day: taking a shower, eating healthy food, driving in a safe manner, paying your bills, going to work, returning your phone calls, mowing the grass. Thankfully, most of your daily choices are on automatic pilot, but they are still choices, and you still have to determine to do each task, knowing each one has a consequence.

Now let's apply this "law" of choices and consequences to the spiritual realm. Here's where things really get interesting, because with spiritual matters, the choices you make count for eternity. Is that too big a leap? Okay, let's back up and walk through this.

Choosing the person you're going to marry is a huge, lifetime decision, but it still only counts for a lifetime (at least that's what the wedding vow says). Choosing the kind of career you're going to follow can have implications for years, but the consequences still only apply to this life.

Choosing to invite God into your life, on the other hand, counts for eternity. From the moment you make that decision, you spend the rest of your days living as a new person in Christ (2 Corinthians 5:17). But you will also spend eternity with God after this life is over (John 3:16).

That's a huge consequence for a very important choice, the most important choice you and everyone in your family will ever make. No one can make that choice for you, and you can't make it for the ones you love most. Of course, you don't just sit idly by and let things "run their course." You understand that God is in the small stuff in your family, so you ask God to use you in the lives of others, starting with your own family. You pray in your quiet moments for your family members. You pray that they will make the right choices, which will lead to the best possible consequences throughout their lives.

We all make the wrong choices from time to time. Even after we've made the Big Choice to invite God into our lives, we still are capable of making wrong spiritual choices. It's not oversimplifying things to call those wrong choices sin, because that's what God calls them, and the consequences are never good.

The good news is that the same God who holds us responsible for our sin is also the God who forgives. Once we've made a wrong choice we can take it to God in prayer and ask forgiveness. The Bible says that God "is faithful and just to forgive us and to cleanse us from every wrong" (1 John 1:9).

As we realize that God does forgive, we can forget the sin that so easily entangles us and move forward to do the work God has for us, which will happen when we make good spiritual choices.

Living a life of good spiritual choices isn't easy, but God has given us the two most important tools we need: His Word and prayer. When you read the Bible, you will discover how to make good spiritual choices, and you'll reap the benefits of good spiritual consequences. When you pray, you will discover that nothing is too small for God to care about.

...IN THE SMALL STUFF

* Since the Bible contains all truth, it doesn't hide anything. You will find plenty of evidence of bad choices leading to serious consequences.

* God never said that the consequences of sin are immediate, but they are very real.

* Because of God's love and forgiveness, there is no reason to live in fear.

* Don't teach the principle of choices and consequences to your family in order to scare them into not doing the wrong thing. Teach it to encourage them to do the right thing.

ALL ABOUT BRUCE & STAN

Bruce Bickel spent three weeks as an aspiring actor before spending twenty years as a perspiring attorney. While he has abandoned his stand-up comedy routines, Bruce brings a lively and humorous style to his writing and speaking. He lives in Fresno, California, with his wife, Cheryl. Bruce and Cheryl are the co-chairs of the Parents Council and Bruce is on the Board of Trustees at Westmont College, where their two children, Lindsey and Matt, attend.

Stan Jantz has been involved in Christian retailing for twenty-five years. He serves as the public relations manager for Berean Christian Stores. Stan lives in Fresno, California, with his wife, Karin. Stan and Karin serve as the co-chairs of the Parents Council at Biola University, where their two children, Hillary and Scott, attend.

Bruce & Stan have collaborated on twelve books, with more than a million copies in print. Their passion is to present biblical truth in a clear, concise, correct, and casual manner which encourages people to connect in a meaningful way with the living God.

The authors welcome your comments. Contact them at:

P.O. Box 25565, Fresno, CA 93729-5565

or

E-mail address: guide@bruceandstan.com

Be sure to check out the Bruce & Stan Web site at:

www.bruceandstan.com